LEONARDO
CODICES
& MACHINES

Scale models making: Niccolai Gabriele
Study and projects of scale models: Niccolai snc Firenze
Scale models photographs: Niccolai snc Firenze
Permanent exhibitions: Galleria Michelangiolo, Via Cavour 21 – 50129 FIRENZE

Editing: Margherita Melani
Translation: Claudio Pedretti
Page layout: Gianni Monzali

Photographic references: Photographic Archivies of the Armand Hammer Center for Leonardo Studies at the University of California, Los Angeles; National Edition of the Manuscript and Drawings of Leonardo da Vinci (Rome, Libreria dello Stato, 1923-1941); photographs by the author. The publisher declars himself willing to pay any amounts due for photographs for which it has been impossible to determine the source.

Our special thanks to the Rossana and Carlo Pedretti Foundation, Los Angeles

ISBN : 88-902056-2-8

© Cartei & Bianchi Editori
info@cbedizioni.com

LEONARDO
CODICES
& MACHINES

CARLO STARNAZZI

FOREWORD
BY CARLO PEDRETTI

CARTEI & BIANCHI

CONTENTS

Leonardo da Vinci, *Self-portrait*. Turin, Biblioteca Reale

FOREWORD

The poet and engineer Leonardo Sinisgalli was the first to make us understand the revolutionary character of Leonardo da Vinci's technological conceptions. And this with his prophetic Horror vacui *published in 1950, when single-handed he launched the great publishing enterprise of the periodical* Civiltà delle Macchine *(Civilization of the Machines), and when in three lines he was able to convey an idea of the exciting and overwhelming universe of Leonardo as an inventor:* "Leonardo designed machines and birds, monuments and fortresses, with the same curiosity, the same shrewdness, with which he unraveled the bodies in light and shadow, with the magic that allowed him to make corporeal what the human face has of more indefinable, the glance and the smile".

One of the most fascinating aspects of the study of Leonardo today – and after all, as always – is that which in his manuscripts refers to technology, that is to say to his work as an inventor. With the first, systematic publications in facsimile of those manuscripts, between the end of the nineteenth and the beginning of the twentieth century, the image of the painter of the Mona Lisa, *halfway between the Romantic and the Faustian, was quickly to be replaced with that of the prophet of the modern conquests of technique, the versatile forerunner first revered by the Positivists and then by the Futurists, an image that was to make him, in the course of time, even the demiurge of autocracy, and, worse still, the champion of the 'italic race', celebrated as such with a memorable exhibition in Milan in 1939, at the eve of the disastrous Second World War, at the end of which his distorted image begun to be restored, thanks precisely to Sinisgalli's passionate exhortation, so that a more genuine presence was methodically and patiently given back to it, no longer uprooted from his time. The study of his work and thought was therefore resumed through the documents and above all through his manuscripts, so that the need came to prevail of carrying on the study of the classical and medieval sources of his knowledge, inquiring in depth as well everything that the tradition of workshop teaching was to offer him. The emphasis came to be placed on the world of technology and on the circles of craftsmen at the time when Leonardo lived and worked, so that his activity as an engineer, that is as a conceiver and a constructor of 'engines' – as machines were then called since antiquity – was at long last proposed again for a critical appraisal aiming at placing into focus the innovative aspects of his machines, with an appropriate insistence on the incomparable visual impact of the extremely original and truly modern techniques of the representation of their structure and function, from the exploded view up to the view in transparency, and from the schematization of the operational principles up to the contextual view of their operation, the same techniques that Leonardo would have applied to the study of the human body, which was for him the machine that lacks nothing and where nothing is superfluous, in short, Nature's masterpiece.*

The most spectacular outcome of this historical and scientific approach to the technological work of Leonardo was to be identified in the programs for the traveling exhibitions on the theme Leonardo and the engineers of the Renaissance *promoted during the last years or so by the Museum and Institute for the History of Science in Florence. It was this event that provided the final stimulus to the new forces of research. The way was finally open to new, original contributions to the interpretation of Leonardo's ideas, contributions no longer isolated or pioneering such as those that in the course of half a century I was able to offer, but constantly informed to the need of adopting the principles of historical contextualization in considering every aspect of Leonardo's work as an inventor. And this was, furthermore, a most effective way to penetrate as deep as possible in the creative processes of Leonardo, in his nature and in his fantasy, in that for Leonardo to invent a machine it was the same as to invent a painting.*

The traveling exhibition of The Michelangiolo Gallery in Via Cavour in Florence, that for a long time has been spreading in Italy and in the world the widest selection of Leonardo's technological conceptions in models addressed to an ever wider public, even that which is not always prepared to compre-hend the complexities of its historical and cultural context as here taken into full consideration, it has now, at last, its catalogue, which has been entrusted to the thoroughness of a scholar of the talent of Carlo Starnazzi. This is, as it should be, not only a guide to the exhibition readily accessible to a vast and diversified audience, but it is above all a reference tool that carries out in a brilliant and captivating way the purpose of offering new contributions to the study of Leonardo and his time through an appropriate and careful updating of the pertinent scholarship.

Carlo Pedretti
Director of the Armand Hammer Center for Leonardo Studies
at the University of California, Los Angeles
and of its European Headquarters at the University of Urbino

Windsor, RL 12423, c. 1506-8

INTRODUCTION

Arthur E. Popham, in the conclusive part of his book *The Drawings of Leonardo da Vinci*, published in London in 1946, lingered for the first time to examine the importance and the interest suggested from the technological component in the drawings of Leonardo, relevant to mechanical projects and to architecture, dealt with on a chronological, stylistic and inventive point of view, but emphasizing the systematical human presence and the effort it made in the various operations requested to position the great war machines or to make them work: "the interest for the machine to lift up the cannon illustrated in this drawing (Windsor, RL 12647) is secondary: it is instead the compact mass of naked figures working at the hawsers and winches, and the sense of energy expressed by their strain, which confer to the drawing a character of epitome of the human power". It was stated here the awareness that Leonardo's creativity was not more imputable to a generic definition of ingeniousness, but it was brought up from the cradle of a long and high scientific and technological tradition that, from the antiquity to Middle Ages, from the experiences of Ruggero Bacone until Mariano di Jacopo known as the Taccola and to Francesco di Giorgio Martini, had engaged generations of engineers in bringing new projects and solutions to the various mechanical devices exploited in hydraulic, military, urbanistic, cartographic and architectonic fields. During the XV century, within the craftsman-artists workshops more in sight of the cities of Siena and Florence, it had been created that melting-pot of polytechnic knowledge which would have become very soon propedeutic to the formation of artistic culture in Tuscany. It was the same masters of the workshops who surrounded themselves with assistants endowed with inventive and great talent, capable to extend their multifaceted competences to a variety of specialisations wider and wider. In the workshops of Andrea del Verrocchio and of Antonio and Piero del Pollaiolo, due to the lively and fast spread of ideas and in a spontaneous connection to the brunelleschian and Florentine humanistic tradition, it was conjugated a knowledge and a well established cultural heritage, that, after a long and feverish apprenticeship, would have put molding on personalities provided with universal spirit and lofty value. Leonardo was grown in a similar context, so rich of ferments, that it had allowed him to examine the yards and the gigantic machines of the great Filippo Brunelleschi, still standing after the realization of the dome of Saint Mary of the Flower, as well as to attend the mastery of the scholarly aristotelian philosopher Giovanni Argiropulo or the teachings of Paolo dal Pozzo Toscanelli. Florence at that time was shaped as one of the more complete and more cultured environments of Europe and every innovation constructed along the banks of the Arno was waited with extreme interest from Paris like from Oxford, since at the shadow of the dome, like Eugene Garin reports, for a particular culture, art, religion and philosophy, it seemed to come true the greatest hope of humanity: peace and unity among the peoples. Therefore, around 1482, when Leonardo sent his famous letter to Ludovico the Moor, in

Leonardo da Vinci, *Assembly of artillery on its gun carriage inside a foundry*. Windsor, RL 12647

order to put himself to his service, his personality of artist and military and civil engineer by now was highly defined. He had already designed, using a perspective space and a careful definition, the war machines with which he meant to astonish for their innovation and power whichever orderer, emphasizing his important professionality and his availability to whichever comparison: "As well, I shall do in sculpture of marble, of bronze and of earth the same as in painting, which can be done in comparison of anything else and whoever wants". To the passion for technology of the "practical man", addressed to improve the productive and economic activities like the problems of the daily life as the measurement of time or the water supply of the cities, it was joined in Leonardo the force of the dream of new horizons opened to man, as to make him fly or to make him descend in the abysses of the sea or walk over its surface. In positivistic age he had been considered a forerunner of those machines that with particular intensity would have characterized the modernization processes that are the foundation of the industrial civilization, like airplanes, cars, submarines, trains, robots, favoring thus an artificial image of the artist-scientist, that in a climate of political propaganda, in 1939, with the great exhibition of Milan, would have been exported all over the world, as far as in Japan where an aerial bombing would have destroyed it. But after 1966, with the rediscovery of the Madrid Codices I & II (*8937* and *8936*) and the rereading of manuscripts carried out by André Corbeau, Nando De Toni, Ladislao Reti, Augusto Marinoni and Carlo Pedretti, Leonardo would have received a greater historical definition, even in the consideration of his extraordinary and complex personality.

Endowed with "archimedean genius", he had tightened relationships with the most powerful political men of his time, who wanted him to their retinue, not only as artist, but also as engineer and general architect. In Lombardy, deepening the hydrostatics and hydrodynamics studies, he would have perfected the devices of the movable doors along locks and canals or would have realized hydraulic meters for the distribution of water, like the one for Bernardo Rucellai. For the Republic of Florence of Soderini and Machiavelli, he would have planned the diversion and canalization of the river Arno, constructing grandiose excavators, while later, in the Rome of Leone X, he would have attended to the exploitation of solar energy for industrial use through parabolic mirrors and to the drainage of the Pontine Marshes, devising dredges and hydraulic pumps. Charles d'Amboise would have appreciated him in the creation of an ideal villa with parks and unknown scenes of gardens, fountains and games of water, but also as an organizer of feasts, able to put in action exciting surprise effects, and Francisco I would have known how to appreciate his inventiveness, receiving in Lione, with the general astonishment of the attending Florentine merchants, the salute of a mechanical lion. Therefore the study of the machines of Leonardo, where the anatomy of the machine derives from the study of the kinetic principles of the human body meant like a machine that takes advantage of tendons, bones and muscles in substitution of ropes, levers and pulleys, involves the commitment to follow the pathway and the development of his scientific thought, that is at the same time a profusion of energies for a study of the history of science, in the demonstration of its most various forms of expression and representation.

Leoni Binding of the Codex Atlanticus. Milan, Biblioteca Reale

POMPEO LEONI
AND THE MANUSCRIPTS OF LEONARDO

Leone Leoni, like his son Pompeo,[1] was architect, engraver and distinguished sculptor to the Court of Madrid, and promoter, in his works, of the counter-reformation ideology, embraced with firm religious pride from the catholic sovereigns of Spain, Carl V and Philip II.[2]

In 1691, Roger De Piles,[3] biographer of Peter Paul Rubens and author of a classification of the best painters, where it placed Leonardo in eleventh place, even after the French Charles Lebrun, wrote that the Flemish artist during his long stay in Italy (1600–08) and the travel made to Spain, would have realized an album of studies of anatomy and physiognomy, showing interest, above all,

sur le degré auquel Léonard de Vinci possédait l'anatomie. Il rapport en detail toutes les études et tous les dessins que Léonard avait faits et que Rubens avait vu parmi les curiosités d'un homme nommé Pompeo Leoni, qui était d'Arezzo. Il continue par l'anatomie de chevaux et par les observations que Léonard avait faites sur la phisionomie, dont Rubens avait pareillement vu les dessins & il finit par la méthode dont ce peintre mesuroit le corps humain.[4]

In a file of the Medicean Archives of the Princedom at the Archives of State of Florence (Misc. Dep., 109, n. 54, f. 228), Renzo Cianchi uncovered a letter, dated the 22nd of October 1614, of Giovanni Altoviti, ambassador of Grand Duke Cosimo II to Milan.[5] In it there was recorded in detail the consistency of the Leoni bequest, which not only comprised works of art of Leonardo, but of Michelangelo, Andrea del Sarto, Tiziano, Correggio, Parmigianino:

Note of the better things that can be found in the Leoni Aretino house in Milan.

A head until the chest of an arm and more of black Lapis, which seems a Prophet. The Aretino says it is of Michelangelo, the manner, and the liveliness of the head is not opposed to let believe that it is of the afore mentioned, – however I have a little of doubt, but it is a beautiful thing.

A picture of two arms and a half, inside a Saint John armed and near a maid depicted of the natural, the Aretino says to be of the Parmigianino it is painting, that is reasonable, but not exquisite.

A small picture of two palms inside one Lady S. Jo:, S. Joseph in chiaroscuro says the Aretino to be of Andrea del Sarto, it is much a beautiful thing, but I do not assure that it is of Andrea.

El Greco, *Pompeo Leoni*, c. 1576–1577. Unknown location

Leonardo da Vinci, *Study of muscles of the shoulder.* Windsor, RL 19013

Two cardboards two arms high of Lionardo da Vinci one of Leda standing and a swan that jokes with her outgoing of a swamp with some cherubs or cupids through the grass.

The other one of our Lady with the Child and S. Jo: and S. Anne both two in chiaroscuro, and of the natural, and both of Lionardo da Vinci, for how the Aretino says, and it seems to me it can be believed them to be, and that they are good pieces.

Another cardboard a little more of an arm inside one Saint Woman of the natural from the middle on of black lapis with a perspective of palaces held also of Leonardo. Seems to me reasonable thing but the cardboard in some place is mistreated.

A book of 400 sheets approximately, and the sheets are high more of an arm and in every sheet there are various drawings glued of secret machines of art, and other things of the said Leonardo thing that truly I estimate worthy of Y.H. and the most curious, that between the others may be, says the Aretino to have found half ducato of the paper, but one hundred scudoes might well be expended, if for such price it could be taken.

Fifteen other booklets of observations, and labours in various matters of the aforesaid and particularly a good thing of Anotomy, and interesting.

The other things do not seem to me to be worthy to appear between the others of Y. H., for that over them it is not talked.

Between the vincian material, that after the opinion of the "expert" Giovan Francesco Cantagallina was not acquired from the Grand Duke, because unfortunately considered "much trivial thing" and not "worthy such a Prince", there were therefore enumerated, in addition to "a book of 400 sheets" (*Codex Atlanticus*) and to the cardboards of *Leda* (gone lost since 1720, when it entered in the collection of marquis Casnedi of Milan) and of the *Sant'Anna* (today in London), those studies of "Anotomy" and of physiognomy characterized for the inter-active psychosomatic comparison between man and animals, of a classic heroic–leonine sort,[6] that for the vital energy from them transmitted, would have so much fascinated the young Rubens, interpreter of the same *Battle of Anghiari*, in a drawing realized with black chalk, pen and china ink.[7]

Just in the rework of this drawing, started from an anonymous painter of the XVI century, Rubens would have emphasized the physiognomic aspects of the characters, rendered as true tragic masks, let alone the fury and the dynamism of the horses, exasperating the dramatization of the scene, as it will be repeated in the movements and the torsion of the bodies of the knights and the horses in the following *Hunt of the Lion* (Munich, Alte Pinakothek).

In fact Rubens aspired strongly to connect to his artistic activity a theoretical interest, founded on scientific bases, so far that Giovanni Pietro Bellori in his *Vite de' pittori, scultori et architetti moderni* (Roma, 1672) would have written that "he was not

simply practical, but erudite", and that a treaty of his, today lost, included studies of optics, architecture, physiognomy and anatomy, where the expressions of the human faces, for the strait tie it was thought elapsed between physical aspect and character, were approached, for analogy, to the heads of several animals, just like in the drawings of physiognomy and comparative anatomy of Leonardo (Windsor RL 12326; 12502), in the period in which he was working to the *Battle of Anghiari*. Pompeo Leoni, passionate and systematic collector of art, had undoubtedly the great historical merit to have recovered the precious patrimony of the manuscripts of Leonardo, that the negligence of Orazio Melzi, son of Francesco, devout and preferred disciple of Leonardo, had progressively caused to disperse from his villa of Vaprio d'Adda, in whose archives is today safeguarded the *Patente Ducale*, that is the document with which Cesare Borgia named Leonardo his "architect and general engineer", with absolute freedom of movement in his lands.

On the 6th of March 1523, Alberto Bendidio,[8] correspondent of the Duke of Ferrara, wrote to Alfonso d'Este:

And because I have mentioned the house of Melzi, I inform Y. Ex. that a brother of the one that has jousted, was created from Leonardo

Pieter Paul Rubens, *Battle of Anghiari* (Copy from Leonardo). Paris, Louvre, Département des Arts Graphiques, Inv. n. 20271

Codex F. Paris, Institut de France

Codex H. Paris, Institut de France

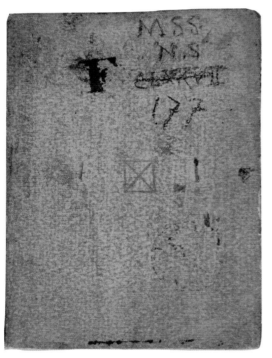

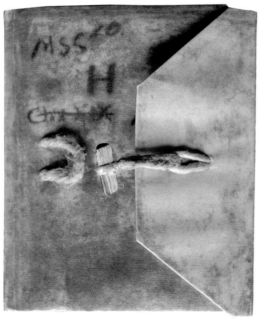

his heir, and he has many of his secrets, and all his opinions, and paints very well as far as I understand, and in his reasoning he shows to have judgement and is a noble young person. I have prayed him many times to come to Ferrara, promising him that Y. H. will see him with good will, and after I came I have replied it to a very good and honoured gentleman of his, 'cause I have not been able to say it to him, because he is in villa for the quartan fever. If it will appeal to Y. Ex. I will make some still greater request. I think he has those booklets of Leonardo about the notomy, and about many other beautiful things.

Returned, in 1550, to his villa of Vaprio, the Melzi transferred there also all of the manuscripts and drawings, received in inheritance from Leonardo and preserved until then with large scruple. [9] An aspect that the same Giorgio Vasari evidenced, on the occasion of one of his visits to the Melzi, around 1565, where he had the possibility to consult the vincian material:[10]

Of these papers of the notomy of men they are in great part in the hands of Messer Francesco of Melzo gentleman from Milan, that in the time of Lionardo was very beautiful and much beloved from him, just like today he is a beautiful and kind old man, that he has great care of them and he holds them for relics.

The importance of the Melzi fund is recognized also from Giovan Paolo Lomazzo whom, attending with a certain assiduousness the villa of Vaprio d'Adda, where he saw the books of Leonardo still integral, he had subsequently to support, in 1590, how much this collection was worthy of memory, enumerating the manuscripts relative to human and equine anatomy, those on the proportions, the perspective and mathematics:[11]

Leonardo da Vinci, who taught the anatomy of human bodies and of the horses, which I have seen at Francesco Melzi, drawn divinely of his hand. He demonstrated also in figure all the proportions of the members of the human body; he wrote of the perspective of lights [...] He planned various kinds of mills for grinding by means of horses, that are scattered all over the world, together with various wheels to lift waters up, he taught the way to make the birds fly, to make the lions go by force of wheels, and to create monstrous animals, and with so much talent he drew monstrous faces, that nobody else, even though many have been in this part excellent, has ever been able to be equal to him.

Francesco Melzi compiled also the *Libro di Pittura*, subdividing it in eight parts and transcribing the relative passages about painting from eighteen original codices, of which only eight remained. At the beginning of the book he placed some texts, introductory to the dispute of the supremacy of painting on all the arts (Codex Vaticanus Urbinas Cat. 1270). Subsequently, an incomplete copy of the Codex Urbinas would be circulated in several manuscripts, to be then published, in 1651, in Paris from Raphaël Trichet Du Fresne, assisted in the version by Cassiano dal Pozzo,[12] who had donated in 1640 in Rome a handwritten copy to Fréard de Chantelou, butler of the court of Louis XIV, and in the illustrations for the studies of the human body by Nicolas Poussin, with the title of *Trattato della Pittura*.[13]

The dispersion of the extraordinary vincian patrimony took place with the death of Francesco (1570), when his son Orazio, not taking care of the leonardian papers, transferred them in the attic, from where they were easily embezzled from shrewd and interested speculators that diverted them to every part of the world, Spain, England, France, Holland, Germany, Austria, Switzerland, Hungary and even to the United States. The first one was Don Lelio Gavardi d'Asola, preceptor of the Melzi house, that, secretly, around 1585, embezzled thirteen manuscripts, in order to sell them to the Grand Duke of Tuscany, Francisco I. But, for the unexpected death of the Grand Duke, the transaction was not concluded and the Gavardi, who had gone to Pisa for study reasons, wanted to get rid of the precious stolen property, yielding it up to his Milan friend Giovanni Ambrogio Mazenta, with the prayer to give all back to the legitimate owner. Which the Mazenta made, but Orazio Melzi was not particularly enthusiastic to return in possession of those

Leonardo da Vinci, *Study of physiognomy in the analogy between man and beast*. Windsor, RL 12326

Original Binding of the Codex C (Seventeenth Century). Paris, Institut de France

papers, on the contrary, he made gift of them to the Mazenta who emphasized in his *Memorie* the negligence in which they continued to lie: "wondered he that I had taken this annoyance, and made gift to me of the books, saying me to have many other drawings of the same Author, already many years in the cases of the Villa, under the roofs, abandoned. Remained therefore the aforesaid books in my hands".[14]

In 1590, entered in the Order of the Barnabiti and made poverty vow, Giovanni Ambrogio Mazenta gave the thirteen leonardian manuscripts to his brothers, six to Guido and seven to Alessandro whom, "Making of them too much pompous exhibition and retelling who saw them the way and the simplicity of the purchase, many went to the same Doctor Melzi, and achieved of him drawings, models, plastics, anatomies, with other precious relics of the study of Leonardo". It was from this moment on that Pompeo Leoni ("Pompeo Arretino son of knight Leone, already scholar of the Buonaroti") began his passionate work of recovery of the sheets and of the various manuscripts, above all intervening with Orazio Melzi and the Mazenta, lavishing them conspicuous sums of money or promising important assignments both civil and in the Senate of Milan, since he said to operate in name of the king of Spain yearning to possess them.

From Alessandro Mazenta he succeeded to recover seven manuscripts, while from Guido only three, since of these he had made gift, one to the Cardinal Federico Borromeo (the present Codex C, which he yielded to the Ambrosian, that he founded in 1609), one to the Duke Carlo Emanuele di Savoia and another to painter Ambrogio Figino.

It was still the Lomazzo, in the *Idea del tempio della pittura* (1590), to transcribe with interest some adventurous passages that accompanied in those times the codices of Leonardo:

But of so many things none can be found in print, but only of his hand, that in good part have reached the hands of Pompeo Leoni, statovar of the Catholic King of Spain, that he had from the son of Francesco Melzi, and it has come of these books still in the hands of Signor Guido Mazenta the most vituous doctor, who holds them very beloved.

It is believed that the collection of the leonardian papers, after fifteen years of searches, turned out to be imposing indeed: 50 manuscripts and approximately two thousand sheets, of which only half has reached us. In truth it is the same Leonardo that indicates its number in the list of his personal books of 1503, with mistake in executing the sum:

25 small books / 2 greater books / 16 larger books / 6 books in parchment / 1 book with cover of green suede / 48.[15]

Therefore, for the untiring activity of the passionate investigator and collector "aretino", Madrid became, after Milan, the place with the highest concentration of the codices of Leonardo. Pompeo Leoni, as it had made Francesco Melzi, in order to avoid an ulterior dispersion and destruction of the material, with great zeal began to order and to classify those papers of the most various dimensions, marking every manuscript with an alphabetical acronym and with a number correspondent to the sheets that constituted the volume.[16] The Leoni committed also easy arbitrary choices, distancing pages of unitary argument and cutting out figures, to patch then clumsily what had been disfigured. The sheets were glued in two large volumes, whose original titles then turned out, *Disegni di Leonardo da Vinci restaurati da Pompeo Leoni*, corresponding to the collection of Windsor, and *Disegni di machine et delle arti segreti et altre cose di Leonardo da Vinci racolti da Pompeo Leoni*, known as the *Codex Atlanticus*, for the great format of the sheets ("high more of an arm", cm 65 x 44) and where it is found substantially documented the activity of the artist for the entire arc of his life. Madrilenian notarial deeds confirm that Pompeo Leoni possessed the books of drawings ("dibuxos") "of the renowned Leonardo de Vinci": one of 174 sheets; one of 234, one of 260, one of 206 and other important works like the cardboard of the *Sant'Anna*, today at the National Gallery of London.[17]

Soon after the death of the Leoni, happened in Madrid, in 1608, his son-in-law Polidoro Calchi (husband of his daughter Vittoria), indicated improperly with the name of Cleodoro, become heir of the vincian codices, put on sale in Spain a part of the collection, while he carried the remaining manuscripts to Milan, where he found in Count Galeazzo Arconati a valid admirer. In fact, in 1625, the Arconati acquired them for 300 scudoes ("sold to Signor Galeazzo Arconato for 300 scudoes, which, like the most generous knight, he conserves it in his galleries, rich of thousands of other precious things"), making subsequently gift, with notarial deed (22 January 1637), to the Ambrosian Library of the *Codex Atlanticus*, of the small codex on the *Flight of Birds*, of the present manuscripts A, B, E, F, G, H, I, L, M (acronyms assigned from Giambattista Venturi when they reached the Institut de France) and of the *Codex Trivulzianus*, that was sold, in 1750, from Don Gaetano Caccia to the Prince Trivulzio.

Galeazzo Arconati, had withheld them in his palace, without yielding neither to the insistent pressures nor to flatteries of a conspicuous sum of money promised him from Charles I, King of England, for having in any way from him

a large volume in sheet [...], that contains the greatest amount of drawings of machines and of instroments, also for secret arts, all born from the talent and from the hand of the most famous Leonardo da Vinci.

Leonardo da Vinci, *Codex on the flight of birds*, f. 6 r. Turin, Biblioteca Reale

Codex K, *Study of compared anatomy*, 1506-07, ff. 110 *r* - 109 *v*. Paris, Institut de France

The Arconati refused the consisting sum of money offered to him:

1000 doubles of gold. To whose exhibition he gave an answer worthy of his great mind [...], saying that he did not want to deprive his native land of a such treasure, and when that had not been of he would have, without other interest, made gift of it to that Majesty.

In 1634, his son Luigi Arconati, making use himself of vincian manuscripts, contained in the paternal library, had compiled the *Trattato del moto e misura dell'acqua*, organizing the texts related to the thematic of water, without asking help to the *Codex Hammer*, possessed, since 1537, from Milan painter Guglielmo Della Porta († 1577)[18] and, from 1690, from painter Giuseppe Ghezzi,[19] fiduciary of Queen Christina, that he acquired it, to his saying, "with the great force of gold", in order to pass then, in 1717, into the hands of Thomas Coke Earl of Leicester and, in 1980, of Armand Hammer and finally of Bill Gates (1994).

On the 24th of May 1796, for will of Napoleon Bonaparte, inspired from his artistic advisor, the engraver Dominique Vivant Denon, the entire Ambrosian collection, to which in 1674 had been added also the Codex K, for the donation of the Count Orazio Archinti, was withdrawn and transferred to Paris, from where only the *Codex Atlanticus* returned to Milan, in 1815, after the decree emitted from Wellington, on the 23rd of September, on whose basis all the embezzled artistic goods had to be returned.[20]

Very little instead we know of the vicissitudes correlated to the three *Codices Forster*, containing hydraulic plans, studies on the Dome of Milan, fables and jokes, acquired from Lord Edward George Bulwer Lytton (1803-1873) in Vienna, where they were since the beginning of the century and giv-

en to John Forster, to be then transferred, in 1876, to the South Kensington Museum of London (the present Victoria and Albert Museum).

Singular, for the confidence with which he embezzled the leonardian material from the Institut de France, it is the figure of the Count Guglielmo Libri. He, around 1840, stole the small *Codex on the Flight of Birds* and tore consisting sections of the Codices A and B, to sell them in great secret with the mediation of John Holmes, added keeper of the British Museum, to Lord Ashburnham (Codex Ash. *2038* and *2037*). Whom, known of their illicit origin, after long negotiations made them to be returned back through the son to the Bibliothèque Nationale of Paris: in 1888, the mutilate part of the Codex A and the one of the Codex B, in 1891.

It is well known that Lord Ashburnham succeeded to transfer to England also the *Trattato dell'architettura civile e militare* of Francesco di Giorgio Martini, with autograph notes by Leonardo. The Ashburnham manuscripts, already Libri, for interest of the Chamber of deputies of the Reign of Italy and after the negotiations conducted from Pasquale Villari, re-entered in Italy, on the 4th of December 1884, and were placed in the Medicean Laurentian Library. The *Codex on the Flight of Birds* had been instead acquired in 1867 from the Count Giacomo Manzoni of Lugo and then sold to Russian prince Teodor Sabachnikoff, which in 1893 gave it as a gift to the family of the Savoia, receiving since then a definitive accomodation in the Royal Library of Turin.

In 1636, Thomas Howard, Count of Arundel, Surrey and Norfolk, Marshal of England, Knight of the Order of the Garter and artistic advisor of King Charles I, with whom he shared the same tastes for Fine Arts, had been able to enter skillfully in possession of some codices of Leonardo. In 1642, forced to exile for political reasons, descended to Italy where he died in Padova (1646), receiving during his stay for many times the visit of his friend John Evelyn, for whom Lord Arundel had written his *Remembrances*.

Sir Thomas Howard was one of the more interesting personalities of the sixteenth century in England, defined from Horace Walpole as "father of Virtue in England" (*Anecdotes of Painting*, 1762-71), became owner of the sheets that form the *Codex Arundel 263*, transferred from 1831-32 to the British Library, after having been yielded from the heirs (from the grandson Count Henry Howard) to the Royal Society, in 1666, and of the extraordinary drawings of anatomy, figures and landscapes, that later on merged in the royal collection of the Castle of Windsor, where already they were in 1690, when they were shown from Queen Mary II, ascended to the throne with the husband William III, to the Dutch collector and

Original Binding of the Codex K (Seventeenth Century) attributed to Orazio Archinti. Paris, Institut de France

statesman Constantijn Huygens, during one of his visits to Kensington Palace. And, from the numerous sheets of the collection of the Count of Arundel ("Ex Collectione Arundeliana"), Wenceslaus Hollar (1607-1677) would have well copied and reinterpreted with precision, though with some licence, caricatures and grotesque figures from the drawings of Leonardo, in numerous small engravings to the etching from 1645 to the 1651.[21]

On the codices sold from the Calchi in Spain hush came down for two centuries. In the Nacional Library of Madrid were kept two manuscripts of Leonardo, disappeared after 1831-33, for a cataloguing error. Inventoried with the title of the frontispiece *Tratados varios de Fortificaciòn, Estàtica, Mechànica y Geometrìa: Escritos en Italiano al revés, y en los años 1491 y 1493* and bound in red Morocco, had received signatures Aa, 19-20, instead of 119 and 120, diverting every fruitful search and favouring the suspicion that they had been embezzled. With numbers 19 and 20, there corresponded the *De remediis utriusque fortunae* of Petrarca and a volume of legal writings. Their fortuitous recovery is due to Ramòn Paz, head of the manuscripts section, in 1964, after solicitation of André Corbeau.[22] But the news of the clamorous discovery was only divulged on the 14th of February 1967 and the contents of the manuscripts were revealed with their publication in facsimile, in 1973, forcing the students to a more deepened rereading of the vincian work.[23]

The *Madrid Codex I* (Codex *8937*), composed of 184 sheets, divided in two parts of 6 bundles each, is characterized by its singular unitary structure and a numeration arranged by the hands of Leonardo, revealing, also for the beauty of its graphical aspect, all the attentions that could be reserved to the definitive writing of a book. The studies of mechanics, which may be dated between 1493 and 1495, and the careful search of a practical application make us understand that Leonardo was by now putting in order and defining the book of the "machinal elements".

The *Madrid Codex II* (Codex *8936*), composed of 157 sheets, divided in two parts, later on juxtaposed, has instead the character of "notebook", of the book on which to spread notes, observations for further deepenings or for the pleasure of personal information, but the most interesting as well for the news supplied on the fusion of the Sforza horse and on the studies carried on during the second Florentine period, from 1503 to 1504.

Probably these are the codices sold from the heirs of Pompeo Leoni to the astrologer and necromancer Don Juan de Espina († 1642), following what is reported from the Spanish painter of Florentine origin Vicente Carducho (1576-1638), that had been also witness of the presence in the Gaddi House of *Nettuno con cavalli marini*,[24] an original drawing of Leonardo there held in the highest reverence (*Dialogos de la Pintura. Su defensa, origen, esencia, definicion, modos y differencias*, 1633): "Allos dos libros dibujados y manoscritos de man del gran Leonardo de Vinchi, de particular curiositad y doctrina". Two manuscripts, which had hunted along also Lord Arundel, who insistently tried to obtain them, at first sending, in 1629, Sir Francis Cottington and then, in 1637, through the British ambassador Lord Walter Aston, but without succeeding for the too much inconstant character of the Espina.

These codices, beyond the exercises of mathematics and geometry, due to the encounter of Leonardo with Luca Pacioli in Milan, contain studies on optics, painting, perspective, stereometry, drawings of rare beauty of hydraulic devices and of clock mechanisms, of presses, crossbows, screws, pins, mills, machine tools, cog-wheels. Moreover they document the studies of Leonardo for the equestrian monument in honour of Francesco Sforza, his activity both as military engineer for the fortifications of Piombino, and as hydraulic engineer for the diversion and the canalization of the flow of the Arno, with the splendid maps of the Plan of Pisa, the fortress of the Verruca and the Mount Pisano, the profile of the hills around Fiesole and Pontassieve and the shape of the Pratomagno or the Mount Albano.

An extraordinary discovery that, alone, would have all of a sudden remarkably increased our knowledge of the activity and of the polyhedrical personality of Leonardo like artist and scientist.

Codex L, ff. 61 *v* – 62 *r*. Paris, Institut de France

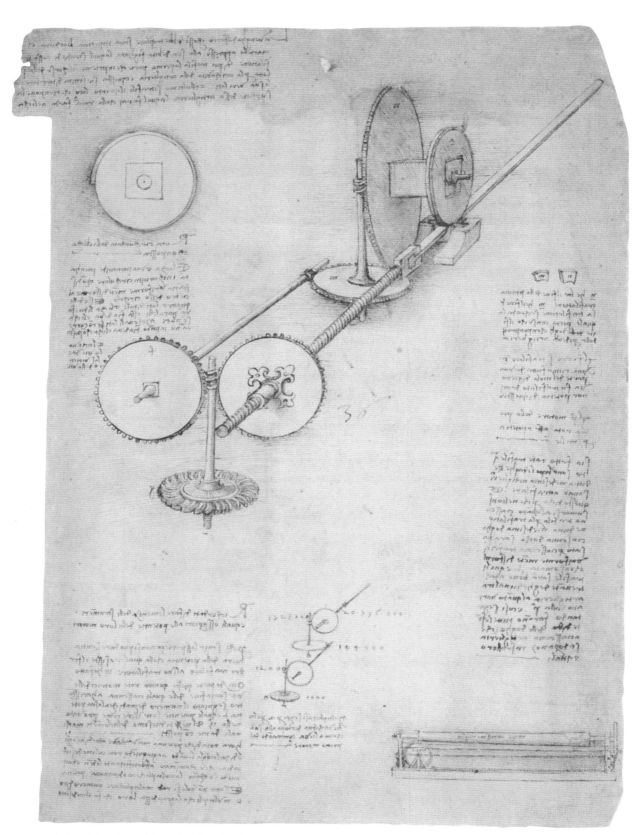

Codex Atlanticus, f. 2 r–a [10 r], *c.* 1515

NOTES

[1] Leone Leoni (1509-1590) or, as he was generally indicated, Leoni Aretino, distinguished himself as goldsmith and medallist at the papal mint (1538-40). In 1546, he was appointed general manager also of the mint of Parma and Piacenza and in the following year of the imperial one of Milan, where he commemorated the victory of Carl V against the Smalkaldic League at Mühlberg. Being "sculptor most excellent" he was "much friend of Michelagnolo" (G. Vasari) that portrayed in one much valued medal, receiving in gift the model in wax of an *Ercole e Anteo* (c. 1560), today lost. He made works in bronze, "worthy truly to be celebrated and to pass to the memory of men", always for Carl V, of which still exist one bust at the Museo del Prado of Madrid, one at the National Gallery of Washington, Kress Collection, and one at the Kunsthistorisches Museum of Vienna. For Philip II he realized one statue in bronze (1553), today at the Prado, where it was made evident the relationship that Leoni had with the Florentine tradition of Donatello and Sansovino. In the Dome of Milan he realized the monument of Gian Giacomo de' Medici (1557-64) and carried out, after 1565, the decoration of the magnificent palace that he had received in gift, the House of the Omenoni, "full of capricious inventions" with bas-relieves and jutting out colossus. For the acknowledgments and the privileges he received, out of which also the title of knight of the order of Santiago and a priorate in Arezzo, he was envied and slandered, like remembers, in a letter of the 16th of May 1540, Iacopo Giustiniani to Pietro Aretino: "beeing he not less envied than well-liked, and well considered from the noblemen of this court [of Milan], he was for envy and malevolence of his good making and of his rare virtue, persecuted from certain gloomy men of his art", see G. BOTTARI, S. TICOZZI, *Raccolta di lettere sulla pittura, scultura ed architettura, scritte da' più celebri personaggi dei secoli XV, XVI e XVII e continuata fino ai nostri giorni da Stefano Ticozzi*, Milano, Silvestri, 1822-25. His aggressive and irascible temperament pushed him to make violent actions, disliked also from his friend Pietro Aretino, which several times had given him his benevolence. Enemy of Benvenuto Cellini, he became it, in 1559, also of Tiziano, to have hatched with his servants an ambush to damage his son Orazio, after having hosted him to his palace, in order to embezzle him two thousand ducats. Old Venetian painter, appointed Knight from Carl V in 1533, complained himself disdainfully of what had happened with Philip II in person: "the wickedness of Leone Aretino unworthy of the honoured name of knight and Caesarean sculptor [...] moved from diabolic instinct has put himself in thought to assassinate him, and take off his life to take off his money", See J. A. CROWE, G. B. CAVALCASELLE, *Tiziano, la sua vita e i suoi tempi*, Firenze, Sansoni, 1974. Pompeo Leoni (1533-1608), operated in the Flanders, Austria and Spain, where he collaborated with his father at the Madrilenian court, completing his works like the greater altar at the Escorial (1579-91). He attended also to the scenographic preparation for the wedding of Philip II and Anne of Austria (1570) and carried out, always in the Greater Chapel of the Escorial (1591-98), the bronze groups of Carl V and Philip II with the respective families. Vasari reported that he was not "inferior in anything to the father in working minting dies of steel medals and making straight off wonderful figures". In 1597, also Pompeo Leoni, like his son Miguel Angel, will be accused in Spain of homicide. See B. G. PROSKE, *Pompeo Leoni*, The Columbia Encyclopaedia, New York, Columbia Univ. Press, 1956; A. H. SCOTT-ELLIOT, *The Pompeo Leoni Volume of the Leonardo Drawings at Windsor*, "Burlington Magazine", XCVIII, 1956.

[2] See G. VASARI, *Vita di Lione Lioni Scultor Aretino*, in *Le Vite*, a cura di L. e C. L. Ragghianti, Milano, Rizzoli, 1976.

[3] R. DE PILES was one of the greater leading spirits of the artistic debates who marked, in the second half of the XVII century, the life of the Académie Royale de Peinture et de Sculpture, founded in 1648. In the theoretical and practical preparation of an artist he claimed the importance of the study of anatomy and of psycho-physiology, in order then to pass, in the contrast between the supremacy of the drawing or of the colour, to the increase in value of the chromatic elements, as able to seduce and trick the sight with their illusionistic effects. See R. DE PILES, *Abrégé d'Anatomie accommodé aux Arts de Peinture et Sculpture*, Amsterdam et Leipzig, Arkstée et Merkus, 1767; A. E. POPHAM, *Leonardo's Drawings at Windsor*, "Atti del Convegno di Studi Vinciani", Firenze, Olschki, 1953; M. JAFFÉ, *Rubens in Italy: Rediscovered works*, "Burlington Magazine", C, 1958; ID., *Rubens: Catalogo completo*. Translated by G. Mulazzani, Milano, Rizzoli, 1989; E. DI STEFANO, *Dal Medioevo al Seicento*, in *Estetica della Scultura*, edited by L. Russo, Palermo, Aesthetica, 2003.

[4] on the degree of acquaintance of Leonardo with respect to the anatomy. This one reports in detail all the studies and all the drawings that Leonardo had made and that Rubens had seen among the curiosities of a man called Pompeo Leoni, who was of Arezzo. It continues with the anatomy of horses and the observations that Leonardo had made on the

appearance, of which Rubens had seen as well the drawings & it ends with the method with which this painter measured the human body. Translation by Claudio Pedretti.

[5] See R. CIANCHI, *Un acquisto mancato*, "La Nazione", 24 novembre 1967; C. PEDRETTI, *Commentary to J. P. Richter's of the Literary Works*, Oxford, Phaidon, 1977; ID., *Introduzione*, in *Il Codice Arundel 263 nel Museo Britannico, Edizione in facsimile nel riordinamento cronologico dei suoi fascicoli* a cura di C. Pedretti, *Trascrizioni e apparati critici* a cura di C. Vecce, Firenze, Giunti, 1998.

[6] See D. LAURENZA, *De figura umana. Fisiognomica, anatomia e arte in Leonardo*, Firenze, Olschki, 2001.

[7] See K. F. SUTER, *A Copy in Colour by Rubens of Leonardo's Battle of Anghiari*, "Burlington Magazine", LVI, 1930; J. Q. VAN REGTEREN ALTENA, *Rubens as a Draughtsman, I, Relations with Italian Art*, "Burlington Magazine", LXXVI, 1940; F. ZÖLLNER, *Rubens Reworks Leonardo: 'The Fight for the Standard'*, "Achademia Leonardi Vinci. Journal of Leonardo Studies and Bibliography of Vinciana", IV, Firenze, Giunti, 1991.

[8] See G. GAYE, *Carteggio inedito di artisti del secolo XIV, XV e XVI*, Firenze, Molini, 1839-40; E. SOLMI, *La resurrezione dell'opera di Leonardo*, in *Leonardo da Vinci. Conferenze fiorentine*, Milano, Treves, 1910.

[9] See J. P. RICHTER, *The Literary Works of Leonardo da Vinci Compiled and Edited from the Original Manuscripts*, 2 vols, London, Low-Marston-Searle and Rivington, 1883 [II ed. Oxford 1933]; G. CALVI, *I manoscritti di Leonardo da Vinci dal punto di vista cronologico, storico e biografico*, Bologna, Zanichelli, 1925 [nuova ed. a cura di Augusto Marinoni, Busto Arsizio, Bramante, 1982]; A. MARINONI, *I manoscritti di Leonardo da Vinci e le loro edizioni*, in *Leonardo. Saggi e Ricerche*, a cura di G. Castelfranco, Roma, Istituto Poligrafico dello Stato, 1954.

[10] See G. VASARI, *Vita di Lionardo da Vinci*, 1980, *op. cit.*; L. RAGGHIANTI COLLOBI, in *Il Libro de' Disegni del Vasari*, Firenze, Vallecchi, 1974, assumes that perhaps Vasari could have obtained from the Melzi, defined as "beautiful and kind old man", some works of Leonardo to keep in his "beloved collection", so frequently cited in the *Vite*.

[11] See E. SOLMI, *Ricordi della vita e delle opere di Leonardo da Vinci raccolti dagli scritti di Giovan Paolo Lomazzo*, "Archivio Storico Lombardo", 1907; G. Gaye, *Carteggio inedito…*, 1839-40, *op. cit.*

[12] CASSIANO DAL POZZO (1588-1657), patrician from Turin, since the first decades of the seventeenth century covered important assignments to Rome, like librarian of the Barberini family, and like antiquarian for the Pope. He favoured the renewal of the Accademia dei Lincei, and was promoter and erudite patron of men of letters and artists, so that Poussin defined him as his "second father" and the Tassoni cited him in song XI of the *Secchia rapita*. In 1625, accompanying to Paris the Cardinal Francesco Barberini († 1631), grandson of Urbano VIII, in charge from the Pope of an ambassadorship at the King of France, who had established his preferred stay in the Castle of Fontainebleau, could there admire in the "Salle des Bains" the *Gioconda* of Leonardo (*Diario del viaggio a Parigi*, Roma, Biblioteca Barberiniana, ms. LX, n. 64, ff. 192v-194v). Therefore, after having complained for the very bad restoration the picture had endured for will of Henry IV, driven from the fear of an ulterior degradation, expressed on the work the following judgment: "A portrait of the largeness of true, in table, framed of carved walnut, it is half figure and it is a portrait of a certain Gioconda. This is the most complete work that of this author can be looked at, because apart from the word it does not lack of anything else". It will be the same Cardinal Barberini to load himself with admiration for Leonardo and, become friend of Giovanni Ambrogio Mazenta, among the first to be involved in the history of vincian manuscripts, in 1626, he would go to Milan, in order to obtain from the Cardinal Federico Borromeo at least the reproduction of manuscripts donated to the Ambrosian from the Count Galeazzo Arconati. The scientific texts contained in the two volumes excerpted from the originals never reached the Library of Cardinal Barberini and constitute the Mss. 227 H inf. and H 229 inf.; See E. CARUSI, *Lettere di Galeazzo Arconato e Cassiano dal Pozzo per lavori su manoscritti di Leonardo da Vinci*, "Accademie e Biblioteche d'Italia", III, VI, 1929-30; F. SOLINAS, *I segreti di un collezionista. Le straordinarie raccolte di Cassiano dal Pozzo (1588-1657)*, catalogo della mostra (a cura di), Roma, 29 settembre-26 novembre 2000, Roma, De Luca, 2000.

[13] The first edition of the *Trattato della pittura* of Leonardo carried on it the following words: "Traité de la Peinture de Léonard De Vinci donné au public et traduit d'italien en françois par Roland Freard sieur de Chambray, à Paris, de l'imprimerie de Jacques Langlois, imprimeur ordinaire du Roy au Mont Sainte Genevieve vis-à-vis de la fontaine de la Reyne à Paris, dédié à Mr Poussin, premier peintre du roy, grand génie, restaurateur de la peinture et ornement de son siècle (1651)" Poussin in truth was not much satisfied of the interpretation that the engraver had made of the models he supplied. See K. T. STEINITZ, *Bibliography of Leonardo da Vinci's Treatise on Painting*, Copenhagen, Munksgaard, 1958; *Leonardo da Vinci. Libro di Pittura. Codice Urbinate lat. 1270 nella Biblioteca Apostolica Vaticana*, a cura di C. Pedretti, Trascrizione critica di C. Vecce, Firenze, Giunti, 1995; C. VECCE, *Leonardo*, 1998, *op. cit.*

[14] See G. A. MAZENTA, *Le memorie su Leonardo da Vinci di Don Ambrogio Mazenta ripubblicate e illustrate da D. Luigi Gramatica*, Milano, Alfieri & Lacroix, 1919.

[15] See Madrid Codex II, f. 3 v.

[16] See A. MARINONI, *Gli scritti di Leonardo*, in *Leonardo scienziato*, Firenze, Giunti Barbèra, 1981.

[17] See C. PEDRETTI, M. CIANCHI, *Leonardo. I codici*, "Art Dossier", 100, Firenze, Giunti, 1995.

[18] According to G. Vasari, GUGLIELMO DELLA PORTA (1500-1577) drew "the greatest advantage" attending "with much study to portray the things of Lionardo da Vinci". Between 1530 and 1533 he worked to the decoration of the sepulchre (the four pedestals) in the Chapel of Saint John the Baptist in the Dome of Genoa and carried out other works in marble for the Grimaldi palace (one *Cerere* and one *Mosè*). Arrived in Rome, he met the favour of Michelangelo and of the Pope, and so he was the author in Saint Peter of the sepulchre of Paul III Farnese, commissioned to him on the 17th of November 1549, immediately after the death of the latter, but erected only in 1575, although the figure of the Pope and the first of the marble statues of the allegories had been finished between 1553 and 1554.

[19] In 1704, when the codex was still in the hands of the Ghezzi in Rome, Swiss painter L. A. David, who already had been interested into the Correggio, reports having set himself about to transcribe the vincian manuscript, but to find it so tiresome, that it seemed to him "to make much, when in four continuous hours", could "read and understand one façade". See C. PEDRETTI, *Presentazione*, in *Leonardo: il Codice Hammer e la Mappa di Imola*, Firenze, Giunti Barbèra, 1985.

[20] For the restitution of the embezzled goods, according to international agreements, Prussia named von Ribbentrop, England Hamilton and Austria, under whose mandate there was the Lombardic-Veneto Reign, the inept Ottenfels baron, who had even exchanged the writing of Leonardo with that of a Chinese text. Thanks to the presence of A. Canova and a certain professor Benvenuti, respectively in representation of the Pope and of the Grand Duke of Tuscany, as he reported in 1869, G. L. CALVI, the Codex Atlanticus would have made return to the Ambrosian: "They walked therefore together where they were separating the objects that had to be delivered to the various commissioners when, seeing this large volume between those that had to remain, arouse curiosity in them to give a glance to it, and having found there some drawings and the writing from the right to the left, that the commissioner sent from Austria to receive the things of the Lombardic-Veneto Reign, believed Chinese, recognized it to belong to Leonardo, and grabbed with their own hands they placed it between the things that for the reason of the arms had to return there from where for the reason of the arms they had been removed". See CALVI G. L., *Notizie dei principali Professori di Belle Arti che fiorirono in Milano durante il governo dei Visconti e degli Sforza*, Parte III, *Leonardo da Vinci*, Milano, Borroni, 1869; C. PEDRETTI, *Presentazione*, in *Leonardo da Vinci. Il Codice Atlantico della Biblioteca Ambrosiana di Milano nella trascrizione critica di Augusto Marinoni*, Firenze, Giunti, 2000.

[21] See *Characaturas by Leonardo da Vinci from Drawings by Winceslaus Hollar out of the Portland Museum*, London, Clarke, 1786; A. E. POPHAM, *Leonardo's…*, 1953, *op. cit.*; B. BARRYTE, *The 'Ill-Matched Couple'*, "Achademia Leonardi Vinci. Journal of Leonardo Studies and Bibliography of Vinciana", III, Firenze, Giunti, 1990; S. ALEXANDRE, *Wenzel Hollar*, in *Livres d'images. Images du livre. L'illustration du livre de 1501 à 1831 dans les collections de l'Université de Liège,* Bruxelles, Crédit Communal-Group Dexia, 1998; N. SCHNEIDER, *L'art du portrait. Les plus grandes oeuvres européennes 1420-1670*, Cologne, Taschen, 2000. The sale of the collection of drawings of the Count of Arundel began after his death (1646) and that of his wife (1654), in order to end with the famous auction of 1684. A similar pathway concerned the *Album delle caricature* R. F. 28745/6 that, passed to Sir Peter Lely in the course of the seventeenth century, was acquired for the Louvre at the Mariette auction of 1775.

[22] See A. CORBEAU, *Les manuscrits de Léonard de Vinci. – Contributions hispaniques à leur histoire*, "Raccolta Vinciana", XX, 1964; ID., *Les Manuscrits de Léonard de Vinci. – Examen critique et historique de leur éléments externes*, Caen, Centre régional de documentation pédagogique, 1968; ID., *La découverte des manuscrits de Léonard de Vinci à la Bibliothèque Nationale de Madrid. – Codices Corvini Matritenses 8936 I-II et 8937 I-II*, La Croix-en-Touraine, 1969.

[23] See L. RETI, *The Two Unpublished Manuscripts of Leonardo da Vinci in the Biblioteca Nacional of Madrid*, "Burlington Magazine", CX, 1964; ID., *The Leonardo da Vinci Codices in the Biblioteca Nacional of Madrid*, "Tecnology and Culture", VIII, 1967; ID., *The Madrid Codices* (a cura di), New York, McGraw-Hill, 1974 [ed. it., *I Codici di Madrid*, Firenze, Giunti, 1974]; N. DE TONI, *Frammenti Vinciani XXVI: Contributo alla conoscenza dei Manoscritti 8936 ed 8937 della Biblioteca Nazionale di Madrid,* "Commentari dell'Ateneo di Brescia per il 1966" [ristampato in "Physis", 1, IX, 1967]; C. PEDRETTI, *Le note di pittura di Leonardo da Vinci nei manoscritti inediti di Madrid*, "Lettura Vinciana", VIII, Firenze, Giunti Barbèra, 1969.

[24] G. VASARI remembers that Leonardo made for the friend Antonio Segni (Codex G, f. 49 r), and for whom Botticelli had painted, in 1495, the *Calunnia di Apelle*, "on a sheet a Neptune, lead so of drawing with such diligence, that he seemed to be alive at all. There could be looked at the sea upset and his chariot pulled by marine horses, with spirits, ogresses and austers, and some heads of marine gods of the most beautiful. Which drawing was donated from Fabio his son to Messer Giovanni Gaddi with this epigram: Pinxit Virgilius, pinxit Homerus / Dum maris undisoni per vada flectit equos. / Mente quidem vates illum conspexit uterque, / Vincius ast oculis; jureque vincit eos". A splendid preliminary study of this Neptune can be found among the drawings of Windsor, RL 12570. The drawing would have been then carried to Rome from Monsignor Giovanni Gaddi, member

of the papal court, as can be inferred from one letter of the 4th of February 1540, sent from his secretary Annibal Caro to the medallist Alessandro Cesati. Here it was suggested to the Cesati to impress in the medal the vergilian topic of Neptune in the act of calming down waters (Aeneid, I, 132-5), resorting for the representation of the marine god to the "drawing of Leonardo da Vinci". See C. PEDRETTI, *Il Nettuno*, in *I cavalli di Leonardo. Studi sul cavallo e altri animali di Leonardo da Vinci dalla Biblioteca Reale nel Castello di Windsor*, prefazione di S. A. R. Il Duca di Edimburgo, catalogo a cura di C. Pedretti, introduzione di J. Roberts, Firenze, Giunti Barbèra, 1984. But in Gaddi House, a rich Florentine merchant family that boasted two cardinals (Nicolò † 1552; Taddeo † 1561) and great collectors of graphics, that with knight Niccolò, who took the place of Vincenzo Borghini at the direction of the Academy of Drawing in Florence, had also acquired at the end of the XVI century from the heir of Giorgio Vasari the five volumes that formed his renowned *Libro de' Disegni* (F. BALDINUCCI, *Notizie dei Professori del Disegno da Cimabue in qua*, Firenze, Manni, 1702), there was, always visible to hosts and friends, according to what is certificate from Iacopo Gaddi in the *Corollarium poeticum* (1636), also another drawing of Leonardo, the portrait of one smiling maid, so beautiful as to gain the *Venere* di Apelle, See C. PEDRETTI, *The Gaddi 'puella'*, "Achademia Leonardi Vinci. Journal of Leonardo Studies and Bibliography of Vinciana", IV, Firenze, Giunti, 1991. Moreover, in January of 1636, George Conn, papal agent to London, would have informed the Cardinal Francesco Barberini that Lord Arundel had acquired the Gaddi drawings, already belonged to the Vasari, behind "recommendation of Your Eminence". See J. EVELYN, *Memoires illustrative of the life and writings of John Evelyn comprising his diary from the yar 1641 to 1705-1706 and a selection of his familiar letters*, 2 vols, London, Colburn, 1818; A. FAVARO, *Padova e il suo Studio nel MDCXLV dal Diario di viaggio di John Evelyn*, "Atti e Memorie della Reale Accademia di Scienze, Lettere ed Arti di Padova", XXX, 1913-14; M. F. S. HERVEY, *The Life, Correspondence and Collections of Thomas Howard Earl of Arundel ' father of Vertu in England'*, Cambridge, Cambridge Univ. Press, 1921; D. SUTTON, *The Earl of Arundel as a Collector of Drawings*, "Burlington Magazine", I, Gennaio 1947; II, Febbraio 1947; III, Marzo 1947; D. HOWARTH, *Lord Arundel as an entrepreneur of the Arts*, "Burlington Magazine", CXXII, 1980; J. ROBERTS, *Il collezionismo dei disegni di Leonardo*, in *Leonardo & Venezia*, catalogo della mostra, Milano, Bompiani, 1992; C. PEDRETTI, C. VECCE, *Leonardo da Vinci. Il Codice Arundel 263…1998, op. cit.* The Arundel House, Highgate, had given hospitality also to philosopher SIR FRANCIS BACON, friend of Sir Thomas, when, hit from sickness in the course of a travel, there he died the 9th of April 1626, after he had written his last letter, that he addressed to the Count for the hospitality he had received .

CATALOGUE

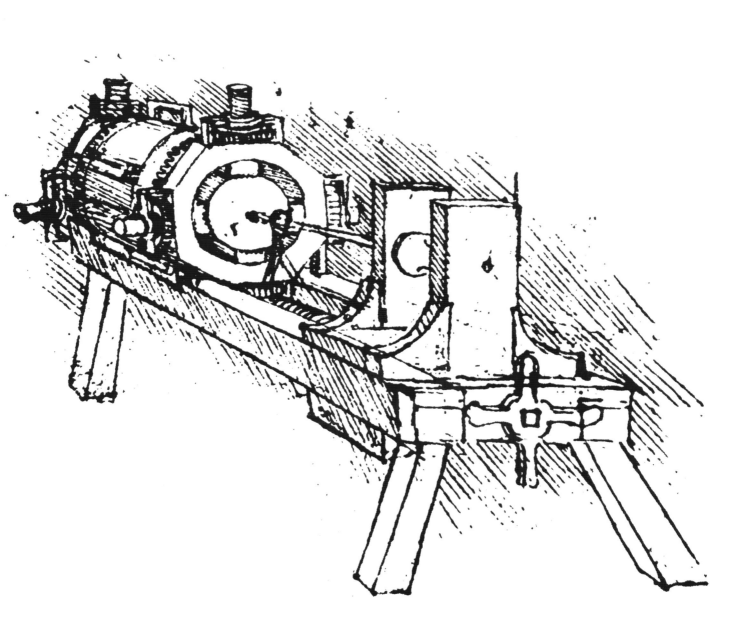

CIVIL
MACHINES

ODOMETER

c. 1503-04. Codex Atlanticus, f. 1 r-b [1 b-r]. Milan, Biblioteca Ambrosiana

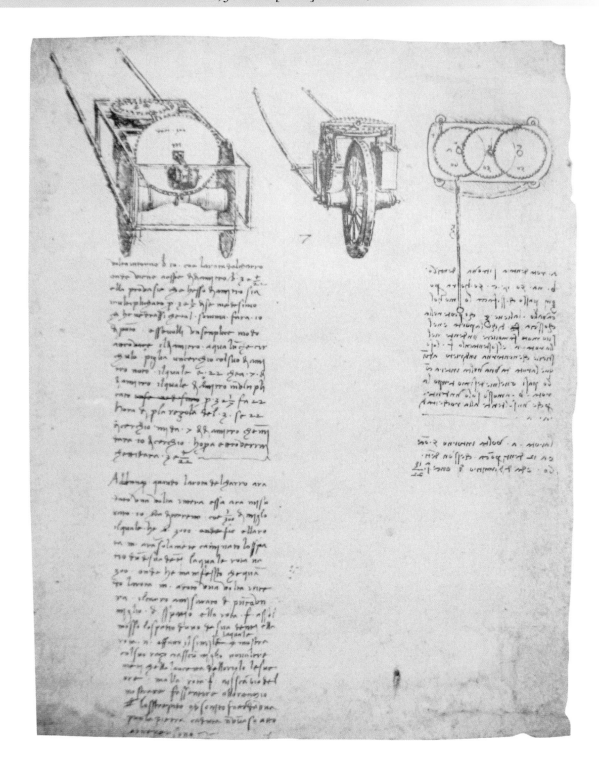

IN CLASSIC antiquity, apart from the common units of measure like the palm, the cubit, the span and the foot, for the calculation of distances there was also the rope, tightened and wrapped on a roll. Graeco-Roman technology had also devised an ingenious apparatus to complete the exact calculation of distances while advancing straight on the ground: the odometer. Vitruvius released a double description of it (*De Architectura*, III) and tradition has transmitted us two models of it. Leonardo, adhering to the vitruvian description, illustrates totally and with a very well planned graphical shape its mechanical aspects, described in a systematic way in every minimum detail. The rediscovery and the use of this ancient instrument at the beginning of the sixteenth century was determined by the new cartographic interests of the Florentine "workshops" and by the same Leonardo that just between 1502 and 1504 was realizing his splendid maps of Tuscany (Windsor, RL 12277 *r*) and of Val di Chiana (Windsor, RL 12682 *r; 12278 r*). The odometer is represented with the shape of a wheelbarrow, whose chassis is moved by a central wheel or by two wheels rolling on the ground. Every turn of the hub of this wheel makes the vertical toothed wheel spring. This vertical toothed wheel, for its part and at every complete rotation, has the function to transmit the motion through a series of gears to the other great central horizontal wheel that

WAGON WITH
DIFFERENTIAL GEAR

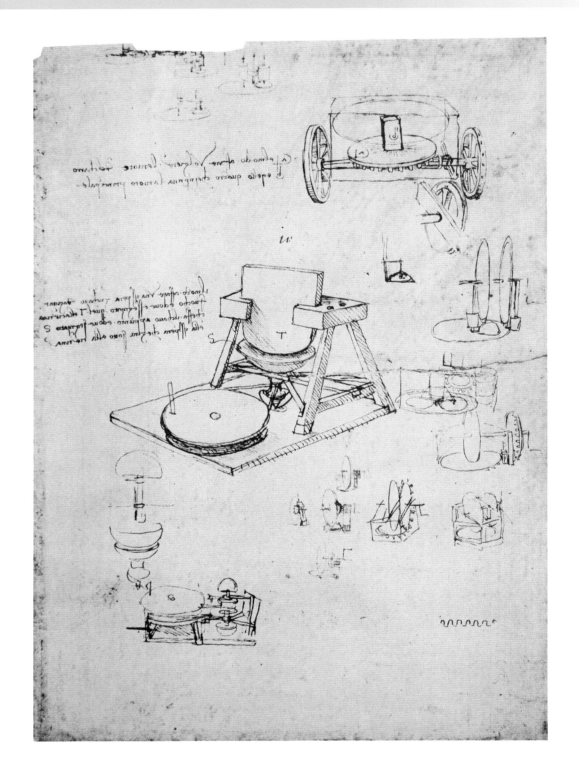

LEONARDO, READY to develop the technology of his time, faces also the system of transmission of motion to a wagon axle, anticipating thus the principle of the differential gear. Such a device indeed was needed to prevent the sliding of the drive wheels on turns, adapting their speed to the different length of their trajectory. It was a matter of making the toothed wheel turn by means of a steering, being that engaged to the spindle placed on the wagon axle, in order to increase its speed. In this way, being the motion transmitted to a single wheel, the other one was allowed to face the turn moving at a different speed.

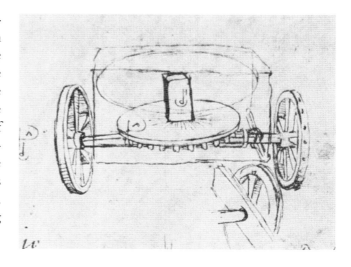

MACHINE FOR THE PROCESSING OF CONCAVE MIRRORS

c. 1478-80. Codex Atlanticus, f. 4 v-a [17 v]. Milan, Biblioteca Ambrosiana; *c. 1515. Codex G, f. 83 v.* Paris, Institut de France

LEONARDO SINCE his juvenile years was fascinated by the studies of optics and catoptrics, acquiring its science from the works of Ptolemy, Euclid and Archimedes, through the intercession of the medieval compendiums of Vitellius and Alhazen. Above all persisted for him the fascination of Archimedes, the greatest scientist of antiquity that, according to a legendary tradition, had rejected the onslaught of the Romans to Syracuse setting afire their ships with his burning mirrors. And the construction of machines for smoothing down, grinding and modelling burning mirrors or "throwing fire [mirrors]", as he wrote, will return on several occasions in his activity as a planner and engineer, in the calculations of their diameter and curvature according to the "caustic of reflection" that is according to the point of maximum concentration of the reflected solar rays (CA, f. 750 *r*; Codex Arundel, ff. 84 *v*–88 *r*). Studies that did not have only a theoretical elaboration, but that complied also with practical purposes, above all when Leonardo, between 1513 and 1516, was in Rome at the service of Giuliano de' Medici, brother of Pope Leone X. It was a matter of realizing lenses or flat, concave, spherical or parabolic mirrors, in order to capture solar energy for industrial purposes, since they were meant to carry to boiling the large cauldrons of a dye-works of the papal State, so important for its economic prosperity. The machine that had to realize these metallic panels, extremely smooth and to be welded together to give shape to the mirror, was composed of four cylinders, put in motion

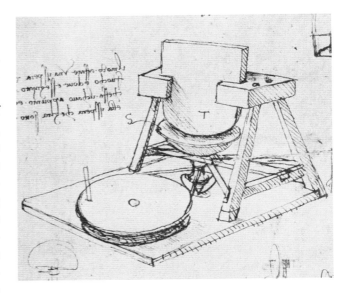

by a crank and connected by means of a system of driving belts: "the base of the template (precision machine) moves to the right and to the left with guides of concavity of two bending channels that receive in themselves two teeth" (Codex G, f. 83 v). Leonardo tried to use the lenses, realized for the textile industry, also in the astronomical sphere, applying them as a principle, and in an evocative prefiguration of Newton's reflecting telescope, to a telescope to examine planets: "In order to see the constitution of planets, you open the roof and show to the base just one planet, and the motion reflected from such base will tell the constitution of the foretold planet, but make sure that such base does not see of them more than one at a time".

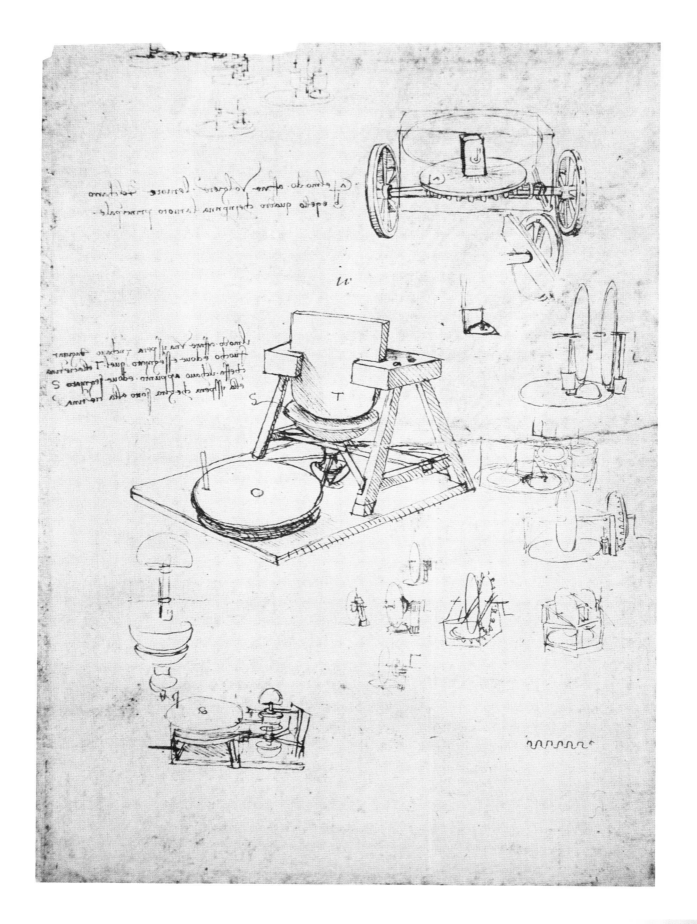

CARVER OF FILES

c. 1480. Codex Atlanticus, f. 6 r-b [24 r]. Milan, Biblioteca Ambrosiana

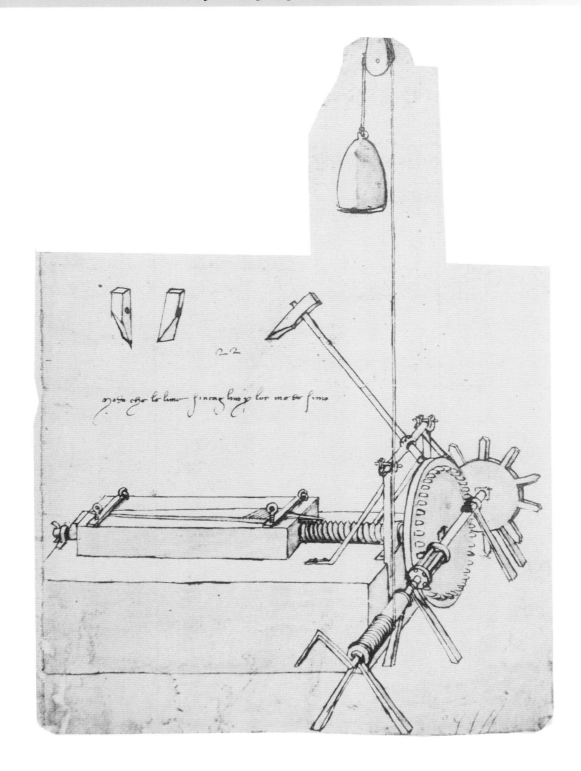

FOR THE high definition of the drawing, made in pen and watercolour, the carver of files machine has turned out to be of great artistic and technological interest. Using a series of ingenious systems, Leonardo displays the realization of a completely automatic machine, accompanying the force of his visual language with the comment of a single short note: "Way to make the files carve by themselves". In his search for machines automation it is clear that Leonardo, in the futuristic creativity of his juvenile mind, managed to single out in advance the productive processes that would have characterized the phases of modern industrialization, also in the ameliorative relationship between man and the machine as well as in the saving of labour force. The description of the methods by which the machine works is rather clear and different from any conventional iconography, since its members are clearly defined even in their functionality. A weight, supported from a rope passing on a pulley and wrapped to a crank for its loading, which is carried out by an operator, falls in a vacuum and puts in action, through levers and gears, the falling and returning of a heavy hammer, which regularly carves the piece disposed on an undercarriage, which is sliding by grace of the spinning of a worm screw.

"GOLDBEATER" MACHINE

c. 1495. Codex Atlanticus, f. 8 r-a [29 r]. Milan, Biblioteca Ambrosiana

LEONARDO TOOK part tangibly and with singular intellectual commitment to the industrial revolution in the textile field that at the end of the fifteenth century and for impulse of the Sforza family interested Milan and Lombardy, inventing some new machines or improving with new contrivances and variations the devices in use. Around 1495 he left his mark on a series of projects and new technological studies related to the construction of machines for the spinning of wool, as the automatic spinners with spindle with fin (CA, f. 1090 *v*), machines for the production of sequins or Byzantines (CA, f. 1091 r), machines for the rolling or automatic winding of threads (Madrid Codex I, f. 65 *v*), mechanical shearing machines (CA, f. 1105 *r*) and also a large machine for "goldbeating", that is for the production of gold leaves for feminine clothing (CA, f. 29 *r*). This complex machine is characterized in its upper part by a series of devices and automatisms, depending on pulleys, toothed wheels and counterbalances, while metal is made to slide on the anvil, to be struck then from a mace whose mechanism is connected with the overlooking part of the framework. Leonardo in person explains how it works: "This instrument has to be adapted so that when the hammer gives the last blow, it touches something that makes a counterbalance fall to pull the sprocket off the teeth of the wheel of the first motion. And this is done so that, the master not being on time, an excessive blow does not damage the work and so that the wheel of the first motion does not lose time to finish what remains".

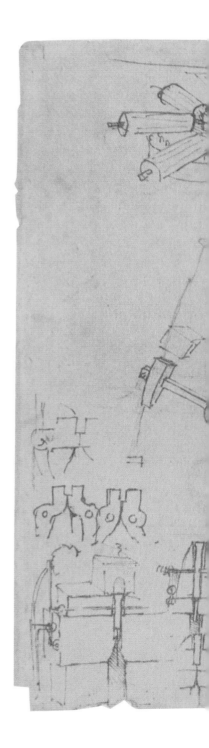

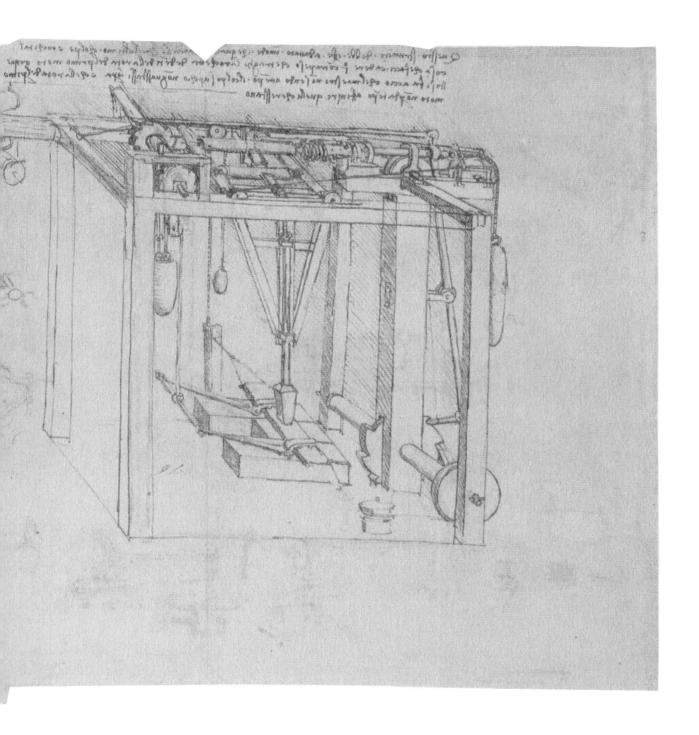

TRANSFORMATION OF ALTERNATED MOTION IN CONTINUOUS MOTION

c. 1478-80. Codex Atlanticus, f. 8 v-b [30 v]. Milan, Biblioteca Ambrosiana

THIS DRAWING in pen and watercolour illustrates on the right and with a different perspective and analytical precision a machine in exploded view (a technique of representation used later also in anatomy), where every single mechanical component is represented in its peculiarity to be then assembled again in the figure on the left. It is a device useful to raise weights, transforming the alternated motion in a continuous circular motion. In this anatomy of the machine, the winch is composed of a lever engine, placed on the right of the mechanism, that with alternated motion, that is going forwards and backwards, fastens the inner stop teeth of the opposite peg wheels, moving now the one and now the other in opposite directions. These peg wheels in their turn engage and transmit the rotating motion to a spindle, united to the central shaft, where the weight to raise or the shovel to turn is joined. In another drawing (Madrid Codex I, f. 30 r), Leonardo gives instead an example of the transformation of a continuous motion in alternated motion taking as his model a textile machine where, beginning from the rotating motion of a crank, it is possible to wrap a thread around a spool homogeneously through the movement of a lever and a connecting rod that operates outside and within its hollow shaft.

FLOODLIGHT

c. 1478-80. Codex Atlanticus, f. 9 r-b [34 r]. Milan, Biblioteca Ambrosiana

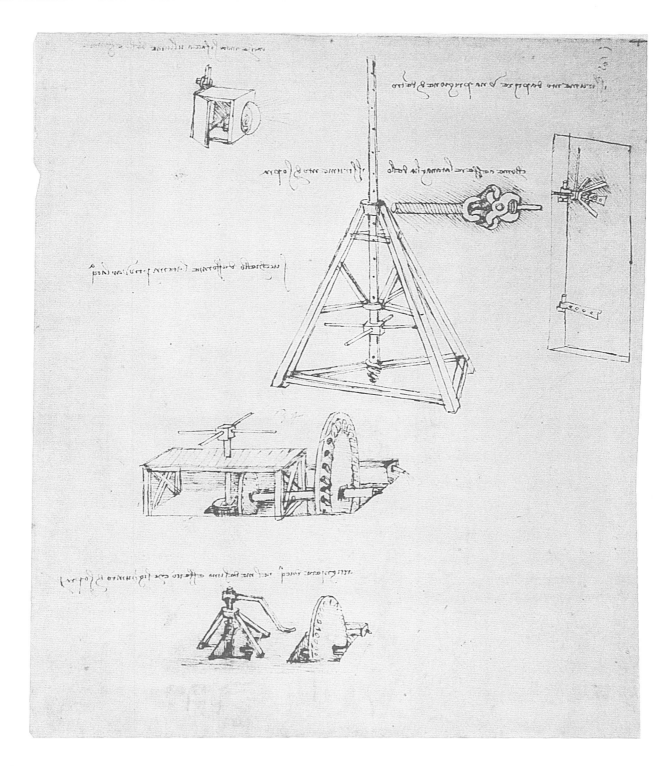

AMONG THE various technological studies which occupy the oldest drawings of Leonardo, when he is subtended to reconsider the ancient sources and the inheritance of the engineers of the first years of the fifteenth century, it appears also the conceiving of the floodlight. It is a simple box to hang to a hook on a wall or on a structure in wood, and, while at its inside it is provided for the settling of a candle, on one side it is equipped with a lens which works as a reflector. According to Leonardo, this instrument allowed to throw "a beautiful and large light", probably with scenographic purposes. It is well known in fact his theatrical activity at the court of Ludovico the Moor, Charles d' Amboise and the King of France Francis I (*"Festivity of Paradise", "Danae", "Orfeo"*), where he tried to astound all the guests with the spectacularity of his ingenious devices and the solutions applied to the scenographies and to the choreography of the costumes, as well as in the surprising sonorous effects or in the pompous games of lights and shadows.

OLIVE-PRESS

c. 1480-1482. Codex Atlanticus, f. 14 r-a [47 r]. Milan, Biblioteca Ambrosiana

IN THE COURSE of his career as an hydraulic engineer, Leonardo took care also of agriculture with plans aimed at an integral reclamation of different territories, having recourse now to the technique of banking up like in Vigevano (Codex Hammer, f. 32 *r*, 5B), now planning sluices with angular doors (CA, f. 935 *r*) in Lombardy and Veneto, now bridge-channels (CA, ff. 126 *v*; 127 *r*) between the Chiane and the course of the Arno. But during his juvenile years, as a mechanical engineer he also devised machines to transform agricultural products. The drawing of a press to squeeze olives illustrates the mechanisms of such machine, which takes advantage of his standard technological application of toothed wheels, levers, spindles and worm screws. A great lever at the top, horizontal and balanced with a counterbalance on its left, operates on a vertical shaft on which it has been inserted a spindle that transfers the rotatory motion to a great horizontal toothed wheel. The toothed wheel in its turn determines a push towards the bottom on the great worm screw placed at the centre of the press which exercises a strong pressure on the olives: the oil then is pressed out and collected in the holder below.

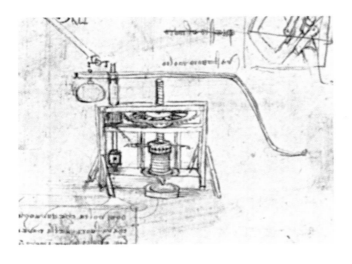

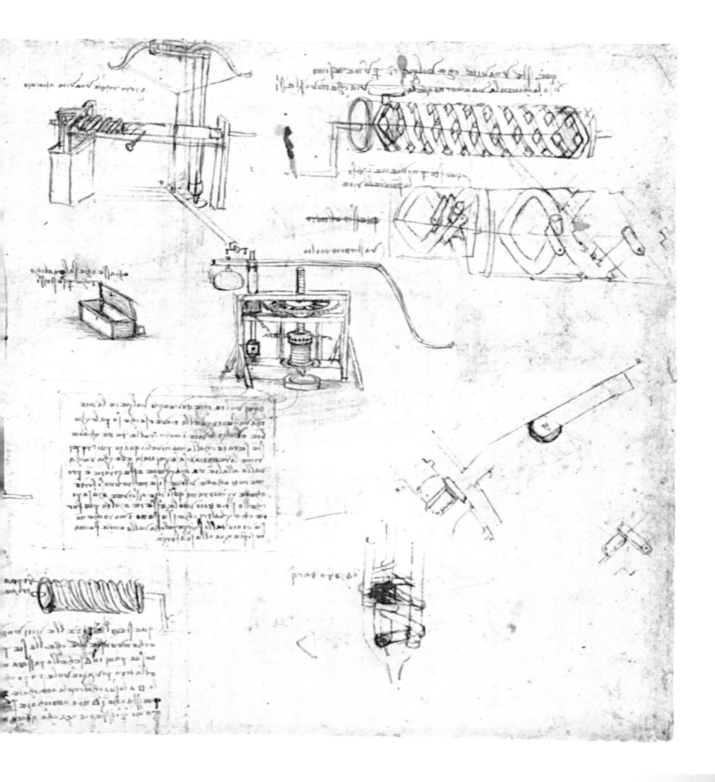

GEARSHIFT

c. 1493-94. Codex Atlanticus, f. 27 v-a [77 v]. Milan, Biblioteca Ambrosiana

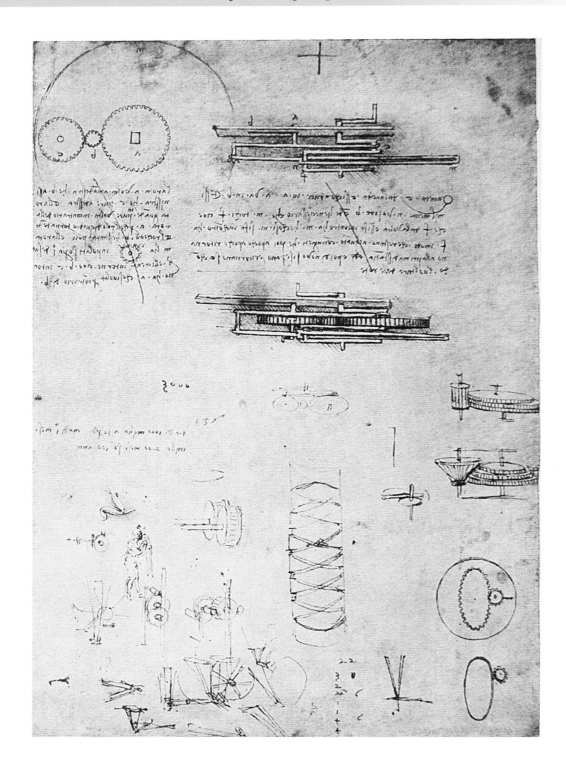

IN LOMBARDY, Ludovico the Moor had impart- the one and cylindrical the other, for the different
ed a great impulse to the development of industrial position of the small cylinders which compose them,
activities, and for this reason Leonardo, absorbed in engage, transmitting a rotating motion, the toothed
this historical, economic and cultural context, devot- wheels which have a different diameter. Each one of
ed himself to an incessant and fervent search of new them has its own speed correspondent to the time
technologies and outstanding proposals of improve- employed in the entire spin. This principle is identi-
ment for a variety of weaving machines or to enhance cal to the one today employed in the gear shift of cars.
the operation of the flour mills along rivers and canals. Without any doubt the study of all these gears was
The two drawings propose two mechanisms designed meant to increase the machines transmission ratio and
for the change of speed. The two sprockets, conical to achieve evident advantages for their propulsion.

REVOLVING CRANE WITH LANTERN FRAMEWORK

c. 1487. Codex Atlanticus, f. 295 r-b [808 v]. Milan, Biblioteca Ambrosiana

IN 1515, after so many years, Leonardo would have remembered his extraordinary enterprise of engineering and metallurgy when in 1472, together with Verrocchio, he realized and installed, after exhaustive studies and calculations of geometry, the great copper ball on the lantern of the dome of Santa Maria del Fiore, to completion of the masterpiece of Filippo Brunelleschi who had died in 1447: "Remember the weldings with which the ball of Santa Maria del Fiore was welded [...] of copper made similar to stone, as the triangles of such ball", (Codex G, f. 84 v). The dome exercised a particular fascination because it was considered a masterpiece of aesthetics and technology. It would have been a reference model for generations of architects and all the greatest engineers of the time would have come to Florence in order to study it, from Francesco di Giorgio Martini to Giuliano da Sangallo. The machines devised and constructed by Brunelleschi, who had operated in all secrecy in his building site, had demonstrated that they could move and raise enormous weights and had carried to fulfillment an

enterprise beyond any imagination. The annotation made by Leonardo finds its place right on the track of this tradition, certifying the other aspect of his education, the scientific and technological one that in his juvenile years is placed side by side to his training as an artist. Leonardo, after having climbed on the scaffoldings, cited also in the famous painting by Biagio d'Antonio "*Tobia e gli arcangeli*" (ab. 1470), made use of the revolving crane built by Brunelleschi and he was fascinated by it. Wandering around the remains of the building site, he wanted then to master that technical and constructive knowledge, and devised cranes of gigantic dimensions (CA, f. 965 *r*), capable to take part to the construction of the dome from the outside. Not only that, but he worked out also various types of lifting devices, among which the model of a revolving crane turning for 360 degrees, counterbalanced with a caisson and rotating on a fixed base, designed for the raising and the movement of materials (Codex B, f. 49 *r*) or, as on a sheet of the Codex Atlanticus (f. 808 *r*), he also planned the model of a great revolving crane on a ring-like platform,

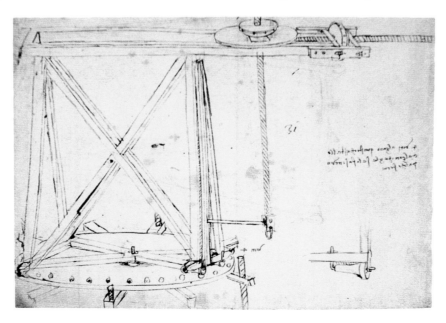

that was able to place the raised weights with great precision and that he called "castle", similar to the one made by Brunelleschi and that was employed for the realization of the lantern, reproduced also in the *Zibaldone* (1472-83) by Bonaccorso Ghiberti, grandson of the much more famous Lorenzo, who was interested in technology and architecture works. He even made a variant of his "castle" (CA, f. 808 v), modified to operate from inside the dome, since it was equipped with sturdy beams that could be inserted in the openings of the walls and with a system of screws that allowed it to move up as the building structures grew ("4 screws raise this castle and, once it is raised, a strong scaffold is built under it").

PROGRAMMABLE AUTOMATON OR ROBOT

c. 1495. Codex Atlanticus, f. 216 v-b [579 r]. Milan, Biblioteca Ambrosiana

IN THE COURSE of his juvenile years, Leonardo had been interested in the systems of the ancient automata, variously described in literature, from Homer (*Iliad*, XVIII, 372-76) to Pindar (*Odes and fragments*, VII). Around 1478, when he was still in the workshop of Verrocchio, he had planned a mobile undercarriage for automata with tripod support on wheels and in 1508 he devised a hydraulic automaton as well as in 1515 a mechanical lion on behalf of the Medici family, in order to celebrate at Lyon Francis I, the new King of France. By the time of his first stay in Milan, around 1495, after having deepened the studies of anatomy, and considering the skeleton of the human body a perfect system of levers and counter-levers, he planned a robot, that might be able to repeat faithfully the human movements, making use of ropes and pulleys in substitution of nerves and muscles, in the joints of shoulders, elbows and wrists. The folding and the distension of limbs were certainly subordinated to the traction or to the release of ropes. The robot had the aspect of a knight in armour and could move its head, arms and legs by means of internal automatisms Its construction, nearly a pioneering study of biomechanics, had the purpose of creating great astonishment and wonder among those attending a court festivity, where it was meant to be the main attraction.

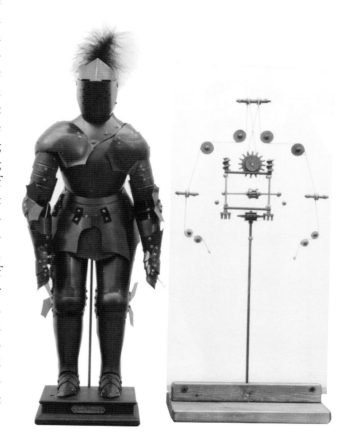

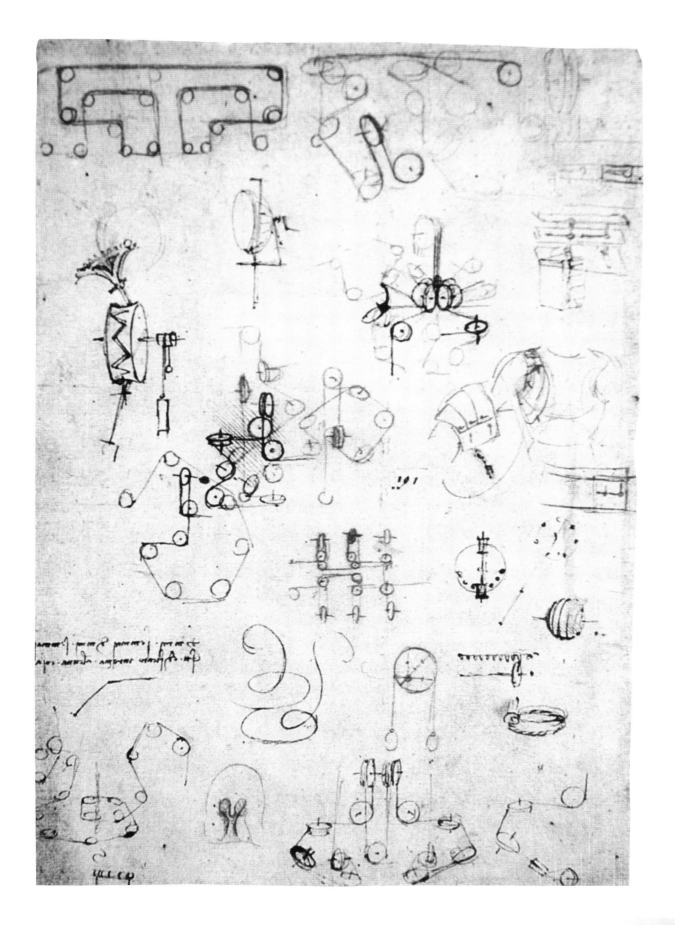

COLUMN-LIFTER

c. 1495. Codex Atlanticus, f. 298 v-b [818 v]. Milan, Biblioteca Ambrosiana

IN THE DRAWING of this machine, aimed at the transportation or elevation of columns or obelisks, Leonardo is taking full advantage of that long apprenticeship and of that training in mechanical activity that he refined for so many years in the workshop of Verrocchio. He reveals himself debtor as well of the technological knowledge defined by the great masters and engineers of the fifteenth century in their treatises, like Giovanni Fontana (*Bellicorum Instrumentorum Liber*) Taccola (*De ingeneis*) and Francesco di Giorgio Martini (*Trattato di architettura*). In this project, he devises to employ an empirical system for the transmission of motion that is valid for several types of machines and that involves both the coupling of a spindle with a toothed wheel and the pairing of a worm screw which in this case is gearing simultaneously two toothed wheels. By means of two vertical screws, which have at their basis two spindles, the toothed wheels push up the carriage on which lays the upper part of the column, while the lower extremity of the same column is simultaneously transported by a horizontal carriage with wheels.

CRANE WITH CENTRAL WINCH

c. 1480. Codex Atlanticus, f. 37 v-b [105 b-v]. Milan, Biblioteca Ambrosiana

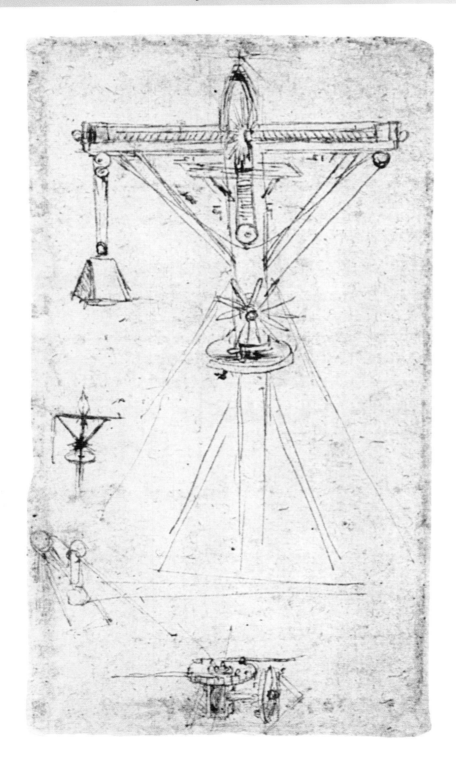

A DIFFERENT kind of lifting device, planned by Leonardo, is the crane with central winch, designed in its functionality for lifting and moving building materials of not much weight. Probably this machine was employed to operate outside the dome. It was made of a long central pylon, to whose basis were placed a tiller and the winch to lift the weight with a cable, while a worm screw placed horizontally provided for its movement by means of a system of pulleys.

CROSSBOW CAR

c. 1478-80. Codex Atlanticus, f. 296 v-a [812 r]. Milan, Biblioteca Ambrosiana

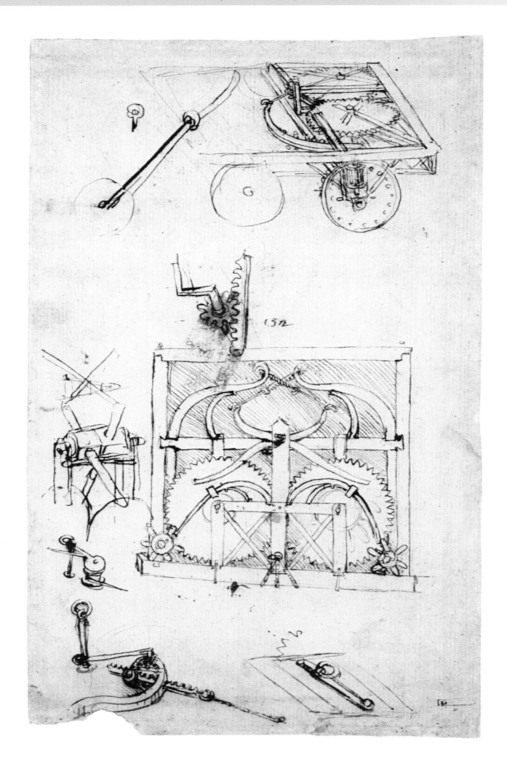

THE TECHNICAL drawing of this machine, though in the limited definition of its details, has to be considered among the most famous ones by Leonardo, also because it has been interpreted as an anticipation of modern car ("Leonardo's car"). Being interested in locomotion systems, Leonardo devised this self-moving vehicle as a probable stage support for the sacred representations that during his juvenile years still had in Florence a great success, being involved for their setting artists and engineers. Generally the wagons were put in motion or transported with enormous efforts of persons or of animals, because of the strong resistance they had to overcome. With this new system of propulsion, endowed with an articulated crossbow mechanism, energy was transmitted by winding in inverse sense the great coil springs, arranged in a drum of wood under the two central toothed wheels, on which a handbrake could operate bringing the wagon to a halt. The wheels were put in motion by angular devices that hit the extremities of the crossbow springs that were connected to the hub of the toothed wheels, and for this reason Leonardo employed an escapement system, that he had already adopted in the springs system for the propulsion of clocks, and fit to maintain steady the general performance without making the spring unload too fast. The wagon with three wheels in its front part had also a tiller, which was used to manoeuvre and to impart a direction to the entire device, when it moved among the sides of a public square.

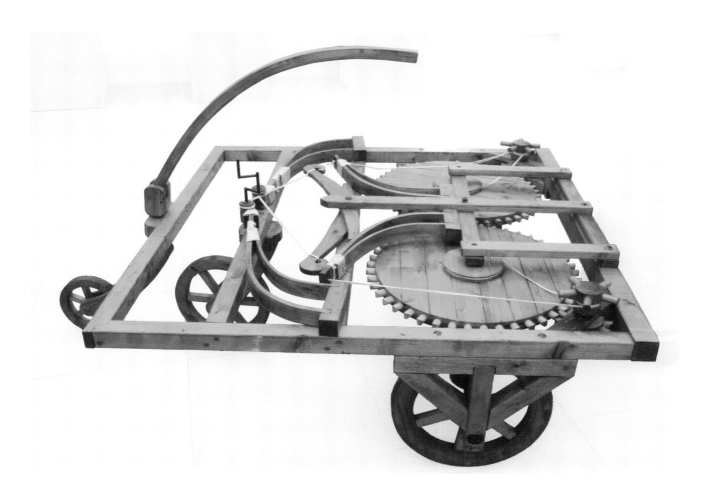

PRESS FOR PRINTING

c. 1478-82. Codex Atlanticus, f. 358 r [995 r]. Milan, Biblioteca Ambrosiana

THREE DECADES had passed from the invention of printing by Johannes Gutemberg, and in the increasing importance taken on from this machine for the spreading of printed books and the circulation of culture, still safeguarded in the libraries of the monasteries, the young Leonardo brought some technical solution with significant automatic mechanisms, speeding up the capacity of the traditional typographical composition. In this drawing, his interest for engineering and technology focuses on the press, where it is inserted the moving lever and whose vertical axis ends in the lower sector with a worm screw, while a great toothed wheel is engaged in its upper part. The press is equipped with a carriage for types which has a sliding plan on wheels that through the mechanical device of a system of gears (moving lever, pulleys, toothed wheel and spindle, which are the most common systems for the motion transmission in Leonardo) makes the sheet go back mechanically in press position, putting aside a manual operation usually made by several people. And shortly after, in the mind of Leonardo it would have come up also the project of a system for printing (Madrid Codex II, f. 119 r), capable to publish simultaneously the writings and the complex drawings of his manuscripts about the "mechanical elements", "waters" and "anatomy", that afterwards, from the half of the nineties, the artist would have arranged, organizing it all in blocks, but conferring to images the dominance over words.

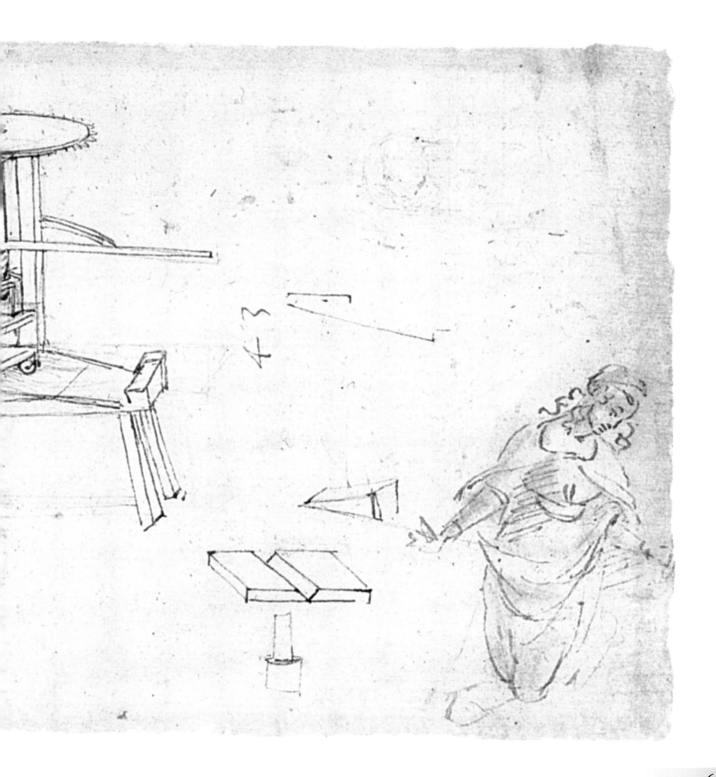

JACK OR MECHANISM WITH RACK

c. 1480. Codex Atlanticus, f. 359 r-c [998 r]. Milan, Biblioteca Ambrosiana

THIS INSTRUMENT, interesting because of its functionality and modernity, considered also the wide use that is made of it by those who find themselves accidentally forced to remove the wheel of a car, is made of a vertical toothed rod (or rack), of one crank, of a spool and of one toothed wheel. The action of the crank engaged on the spool brings about that the spool, gearing on the larger toothed wheel, makes the toothed wheel move allowing it to go up or to come down along the rack. Conceived with the technical and scientific attitude typical of the time, where practical problems were never separated from a theoretical idea, this device remarkably favours the movement of a load from a lower level upwards, with a great saving of energy, since it transforms circular motion into rectilinear motion.

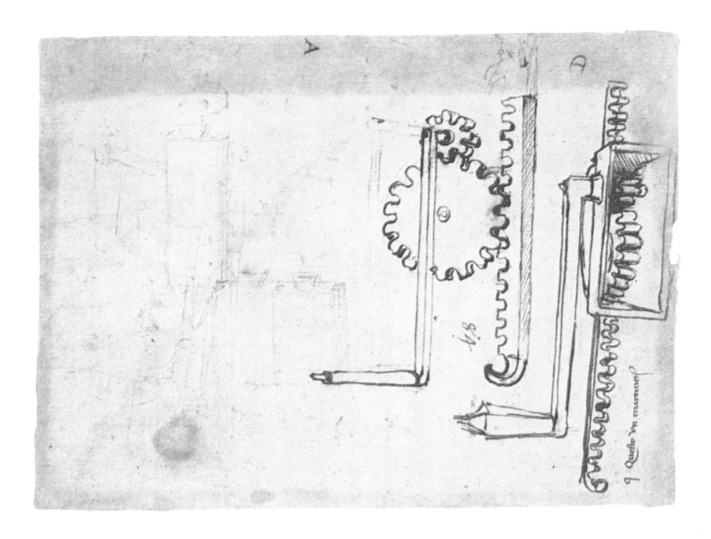

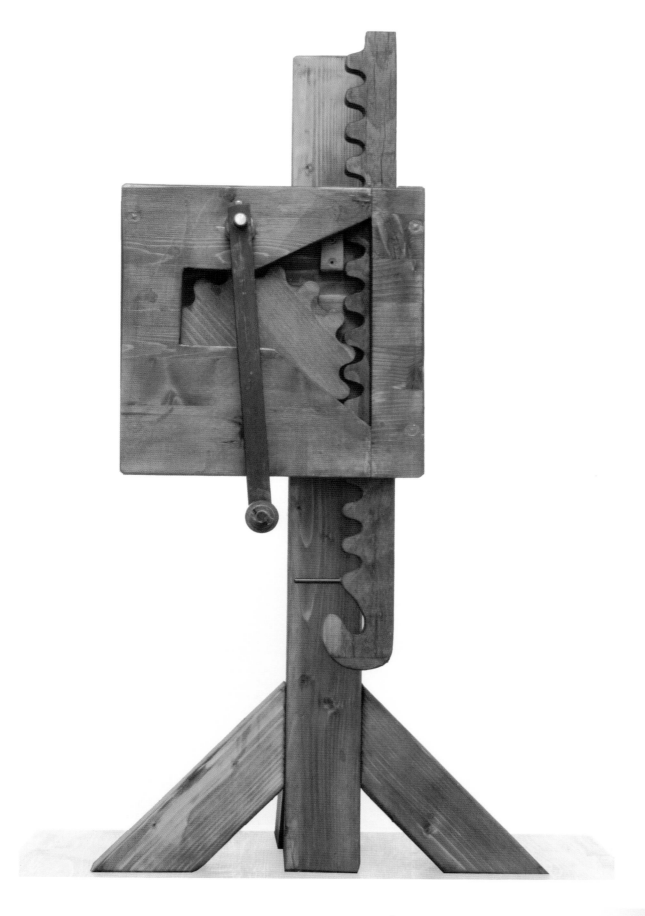

WINCH WITH MANY SPEEDS

c. 1478. Codex Atlanticus, f. 391 v-b [1083 v]. Milan, Biblioteca Ambrosiana

LEONARDO MET the fascinating world of machines and of the related technological problems in the workshop of Verrocchio. But he did not fail to refer himself to the world of the engineeristic tradition of Brunelleschi, from whom he copied his extraordinary machines and gears, developing them with great confidence in other drawings. Attracted by the combination of those several devices and by their mechanisms, he studied the structure and the advantages brought about by a great winch, designed to raise enormous burdens up to remarkable heights, where gigantic lifting devices and revolving cranes would have put them in position with extreme perfection. The winch, operating from the ground, is made up of a double horizontal shaft where to wrap sturdy ropes, while a device constituted by a worm screw and two horizontal wheels, that are geared in alternate way with the pegs of the drum of the shafts and that make them turn with different powers, allows the realization of a motion with a continuous cycle, making the material to come down or to raise without any interruption.

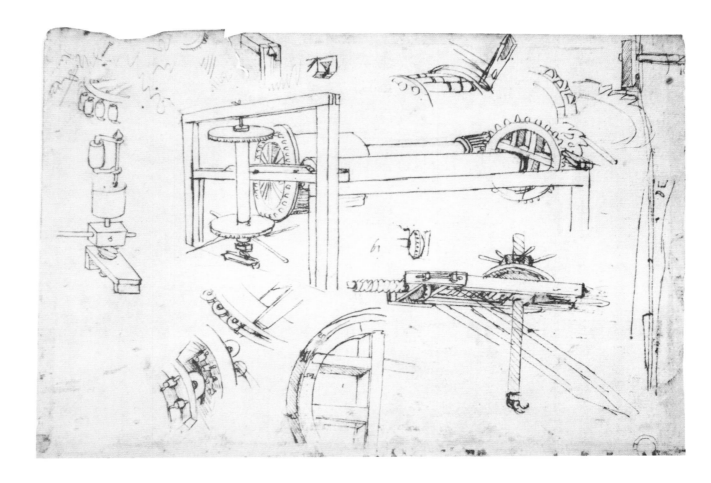

ROOM
OF MIRRORS

c. 1486. Codex B, f. 28 r. Paris, Institut de France

LEONARDO, PLANNING his room of mirrors, seems to know and to consider the assumptions that are at the foundations of the reflection law (the angle of incidence is equal to the reflection angle). Interested in the play of the multiplication of images produced by mirrors, he writes:

"If you will make eight flat mirrors and each one is 2 arms wide and 3 [arms] high and they are put in a circle so that they make one [room] with 8 faces, that will go round for 16 arms, and its diameter must be of 5 arms, the man that will find himself there, will be able to see every part [of himself] endless times. If there will be 4 mirrors put in square, that will still be good".

In fact, putting an object in position between two flat and parallel mirrors, the first mirror produces a symmetrical image, that has the same dimensions of the object, since in a flat reflecting surface an object is neither magnified nor reduced. This first image in its turn produces a second image due to the other mirror and symmetrical with regard to the last one, in order then to work in its turn as a starting source for the first mirror, with the production of a third image with regard to the first mirror and so on without end. Of course the following multiple images turn out to be placed farther and farther with regard to the reflecting surface and for this reason, being seen under a lesser angle, they appear smaller, even though they have the same dimensions of the starting source. If mirrors are arranged, as Leonardo says, according to a square or octagonal geometry there will be several couples of mirrors, whose effects will be further multiplied according to the patterns previously described.

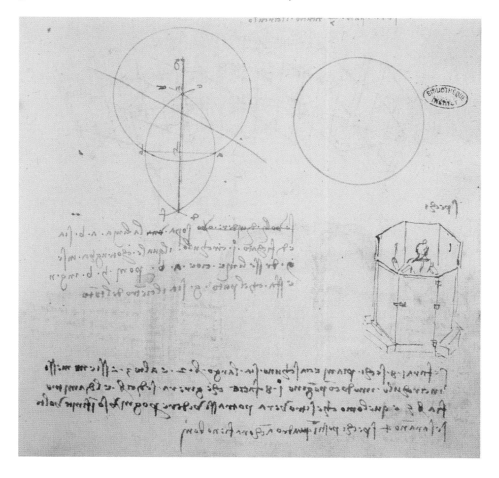

VERTICAL AND
HORIZONTAL DRILL

c. 1485. Codex B, f. 47 v. Paris, Institut de France; *c. 1495-97.* Codex Atlanticus, *f. 393 r [1089 r].* Milan, Biblioteca Ambrosiana

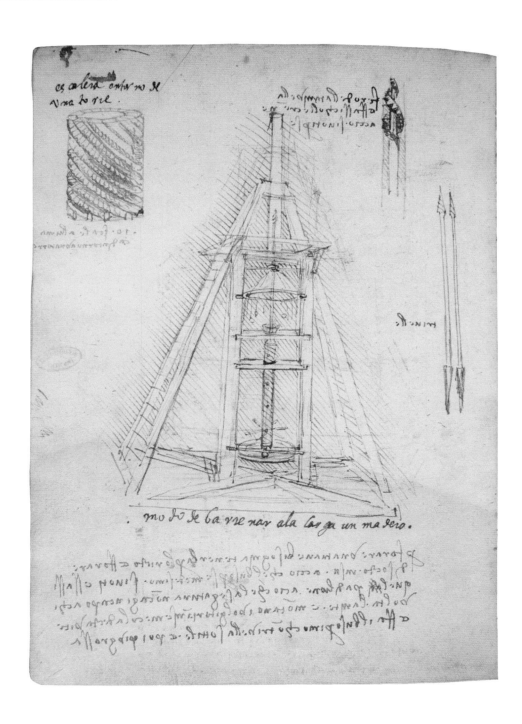

THE DRILL, also, defined here with great graphic and functional completeness, is part of the interests that Leonardo reserved to the systematic exploration of the several inventions that have by tradition involved, since ancient times, the labour world as well as the world of hydraulic engineering. It was a widespread device of great usefulness, since it was employed for the realization of wells in clayey and soft soils, so as to draw water from the water-bearing strata at various depths. The well was in general dug with a circular section and its walls were made waterproof with a covering of mortar masonry. The shaft of the drill, supported from a triangular frame, allowed to perforate soil through the spin of a worm screw, described as an "auger to pierce earth in order to find water", and it was set in action from a winch pushed with force from some men on a platform. Leonardo will plan also other types of drill, as the one to pierce tree trunks (Ms. B, f. 47 *v*), used as water pipes, but in that case the device will operate by means of a screw from the bottom upwards.

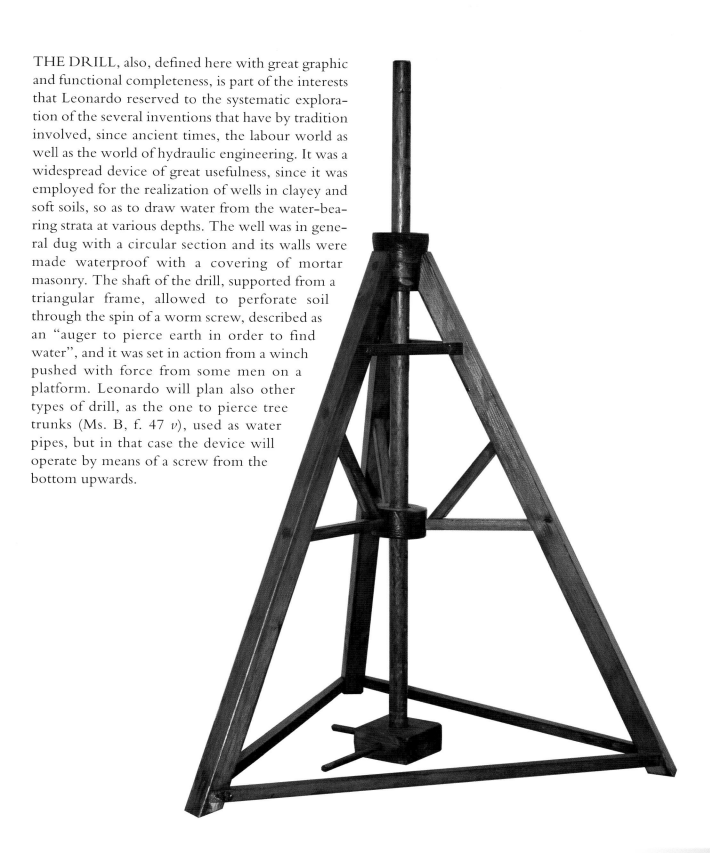

FOSSILS

c. 1498-9 and c. 1508-9. Codex I, ff. 24 v, 25 r; Codex F, f.80 r. Paris, Institut de France

PALAEONTOLOGY IS a historiographic science that has as its end the reconstruction of the history of life through the analysis of particular documents: fossils, that is the study of the petrified remains of organisms that lived in a remote past. Leonardo can, with good reason, be considered the father of this modern science, since he was the first to understand, though adhering himself to the creationistic thesis, the true nature of fossils, and he was the first who began to observe those biostratinomic phenomena to which the organic remains go and encounter after their death, and he was the first to consider the ecological relations that the organisms establish between them and their environment, and he was the first to have a clear idea on the same processes of fossilization (Codex F, f. 79 v). The organic nature of fossils had been recognized even by the philosophers of ancient Greece, by Xenophanes, Pithagoras, Herodotus and

Theophrastus, that had considered them to be an effect of a "vis plastica" or of a "lusus naturae". In the Middle Ages, the presence of remains of sea animals on the hill slopes and mounts had been instead thought to be an unquestionable assessment of the truthfulness of the biblical story of the universal Flood. And a theory of the Deluge asserted and developed itself thanks to the work of Ristoro d'Arezzo (*Composizione del mondo*, II, 5, 8), in order then to be over and over supported until the seventeenth century. Leonardo, that had developed his interest in the fossil sea organisms ("shells and corals"), since the realiza-

tion of the "great horse of Milan" (Codex Hammer, f. 9 v, 9B), rejected with decision such theory on the basis of careful reasoning of taphonomic (Codex Hammer, f. 9 v, 9B), stratigraphic and sedimentological (Codex Hammer, f. 10 r, 10 A) character. Among the fossil sea organisms, those that mainly captured his attention were certain types of gasteropods and of ammonites, given the singular structure of helicoidal torsion of the architecture of their shell. This diversified typology of natural spiral shapes will be preferred by the artist also to adorn the helms and the shoulder-plates of the knights of the *Battle of Anghiari* (1503-04).

ESCALATOR

GEARS AND MECHANISMS FOR THE TRANSMISSION OF MOTION

c. 1487-90. Codex Forster I², f. 46 v. London, Victoria and Albert Museum; *c. 1493-94. Codex H, f. 86 v.* Paris Institut de France; *c. 1497. Madrid Codex I, ff. 13 r, 17 v.* Madrid, Biblioteca Nacional

THE COUPLING of the worm screw to the toothed wheel constitutes for Leonardo a gear of great effectiveness (Madrid Codex I, f. 17 *v*), superior to the mechanism of the spindle-toothed wheel (Codex H, f. 86 v), widely used as well by the artist and scientist for the transmission of the rotating motion in his machines, but of lesser reliability, above all if the spindle is out of the axis as regards the peg wheel, since "the teeth of K are consumed twice because they have two motions, crosswise and sideways". On the contrary, the worm wheel has a concave and helicoidal shape that concurs to engage and to gear inside more than one teeth of the wheel. By determining therefore the distribution of force in more points, the imprinting of a circular motion to the wheel diminishes the risk of break, since it makes greater the resistance of the wheel and guarantees over its reliability, because it "takes many teeth of the wheel", even if it has to move large weights. Such a device was applied by Leonardo to the mechanical structure of the escalator, that taking advantage of these mechanisms could be lengthened or shortened in dependency of the single and various situations both in civil and military field.

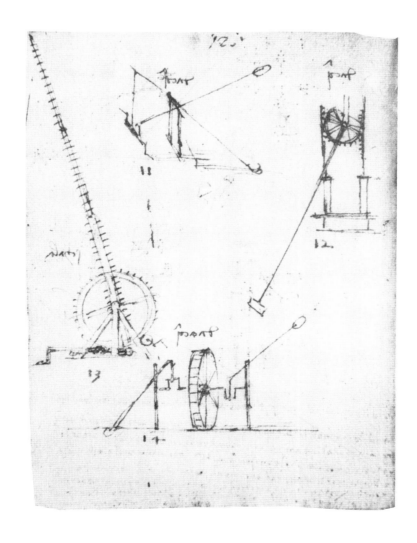

CAM HAMMER

c. 1497. Madrid Codex I, f. 6 v. Madrid, Biblioteca Nacional

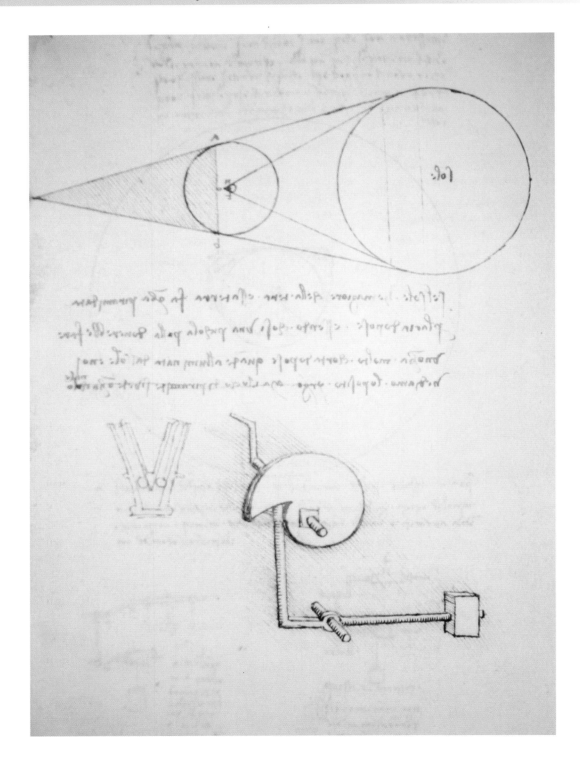

A CAM is commonly defined as a mechanical organ designed for the transformation of rotatory motion in back-and-forth or up-and-down intermittent motion. Leonardo, interested in the automatism that could be used while at work, applied it, as a simple device, to the percussion of a hammer on an anvil. One crank, which has its fulcrum directly in the cam, activates its rotatory movement. The cam, that has a circular profile suddenly broken and on which is engaged the lever, to which is connected a hammer, on turning makes the lever tilt, and after that the lever returns to the initial departure position when the cams have completed their turn. Only then, because of the gravity law, the lever makes the mallet fall heavily on the anvil, starting an automation process, which alleviates hard work and saves energy to human activity.

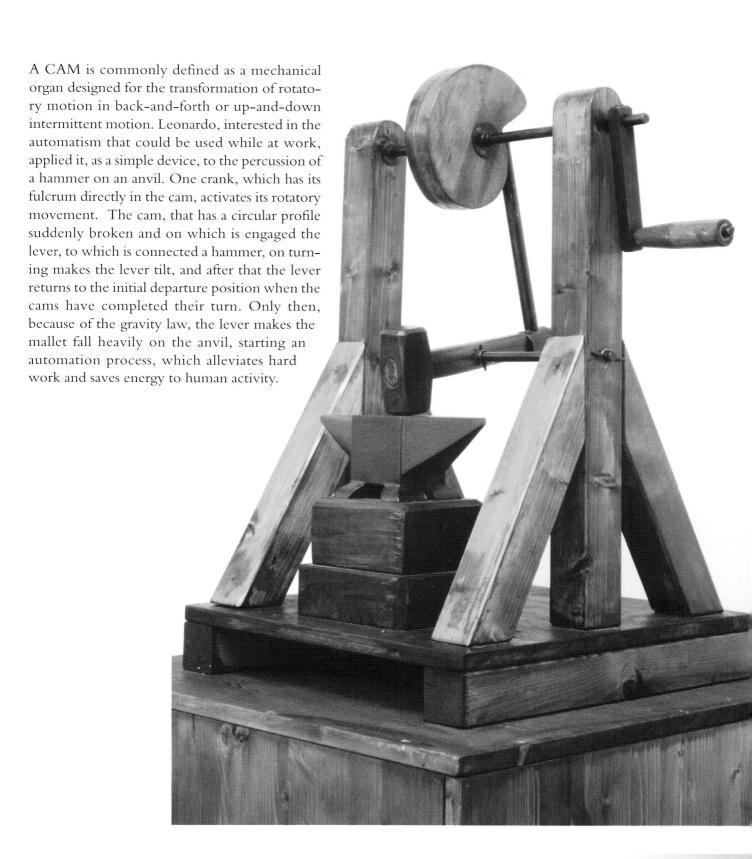

CHAIN

c. 1497. Madrid Codex I, f. 10 r. Madrid, Biblioteca Nacional

THE EMPLOYMENT of chains, considered the multiplicity of the variants examined, has been used with great attention by Leonardo for the transmission of rotatory motion, since according to his survey it turned out to be more favourable than the most common use of the rope, also in relation to the raising of heavy loads. Theoretically, chains, placed on far-away among them toothed wheels lying on the same plane, could transmit a continuous motion, but the angular and squared shape of the teeth, that sometimes he draws more rounded off in order to facilitate their sliding, as well as the weights hanging at the extremities suggest their employment for the transmission of a discontinuous motion to a single toothed wheel, that might be appropriate to spring release mechanisms, as in those of clocks.

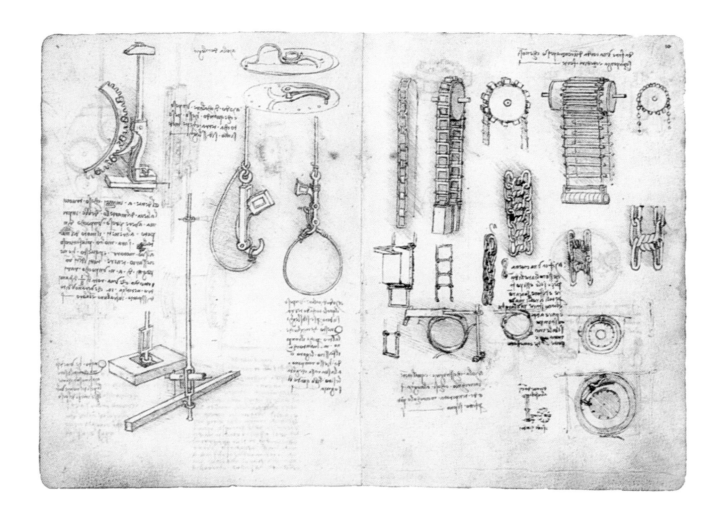

BALL BEARINGS

c. 1497. Madrid Codex I, f. 20 v. Madrid, Biblioteca Nacional

FOR CENTURIES, the problem of friction, produced from the several solicitations that the machine endured, up to being prevented in its functionality, above all at the occurrence of a heavy load, it was closely connected to the transmission of motion. Therefore, in order to optimize the performance of the machines in motion, limiting the wearing effect of friction, Leonardo, driven in his search of planner and engineer to the solution of practical problems, devised with great advance regarding modern mechanics the ball bearings.

An extraordinary drawing illustrates its system and structure, proposing both its view in plant and the transversal section, for any potential construction of it. The flowing ring of the ball bearing is made of eight spheres, with free motion, spaced out and embedded between as many concave spools, rotat-ing instead on themselves and perfectly adherent to them. Leonardo employed this device, on the occasion of the theatrical representation of Poliziano's *"Favola di Orfeo"* for Charles d'Amboise in Milan. It was a matter of realizing a great revolving stage in wood, rotating on a central axis and build so as to link up the proscenium with the backstage, but already famous in its structure since antiquity, since it was described by Pliny the Elder as theatre of Curion (*Naturalis Historia*, XXXVI, 24). Once constituted the two hemicycles, employing the ball bearings, it was possible to carry out a double theatrical representation at the same time.

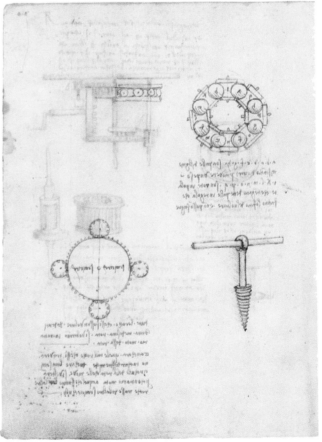

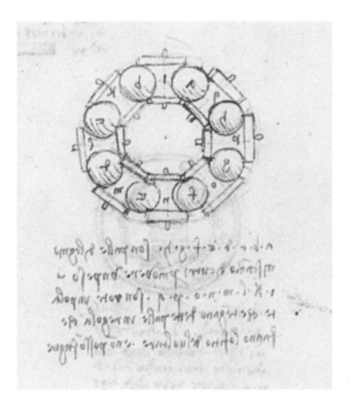

MACHINE FOR RAISING OBJECTS OF GREAT HEIGHT

c. 1497. Madrid Codex, f. 43 r. Madrid, Biblioteca Nacional

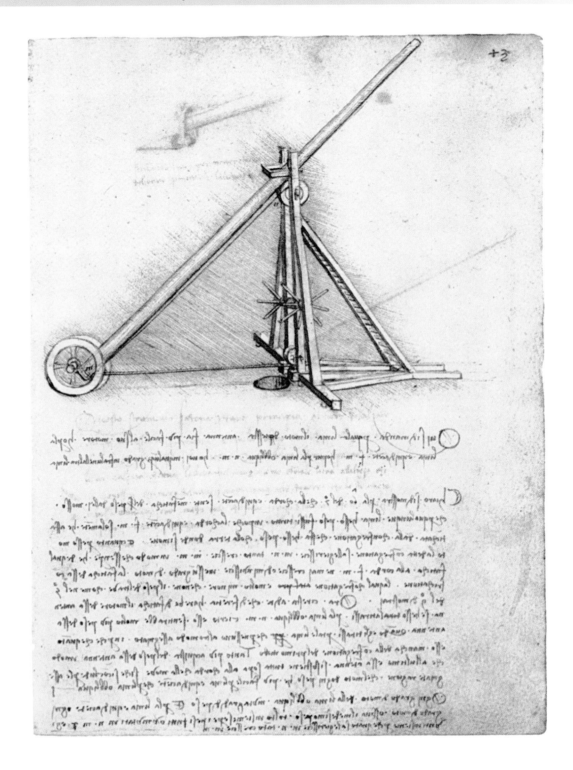

ALSO IN the study of the machine to raise long weights, columns or large devices, Leonardo inverts the praxis of its time, favouring a radical and systematic study of the single "mechanical elements", so that, in sight of the construction of structures and mechanical apparatuses, they might constitute an entirety, a synthesis of theory and practice. Therefore in an assumption that requires studies of dynamics, statics and geometry, together with the practical aspects of the mechanical project in itself, he writes: "[...] the motion of every weight is easier through the equidistant line than for the oblique line". The long perch is lifted, from the base, by means of a rope, connected horizontally to the roll of a winch. The same wheels have a part in reducing friction and in diminishing the hard work to employ.

STUDY OF LEVERS AND SPRINGS IN ORDER TO PULL

c. 1497. Madrid Codex I, f. 44 v. Madrid, Biblioteca Nacional

IN THESE two drawings, so clean and specified up to minimums details, Leonardo represents, in plant and in elevation, the machine to pull at the same time some rods or perches. And, to complete the description and the mechanisms of such construction and its operation, he adds: "You must know that the wheels towards the centre are mobile, those towards the greater circle can be lifted. And in the turning of the winch it is made a circular movement, because the small wheels inside approach the small wheels outside and they bring along all that is tied up to them". He imagines that the perches, dislocated along the inner perimeter of a platform and arranged on a pivot, are subordinated to the action of a double aureole of pulleys, fixed the external, and mobile, even though connected to the perch, the inner ones. A very stiff cable, passing among them and wrapped on the cylinders of a winch, transmits the necessary force, so that all the perches are simultaneously and tidily raised.

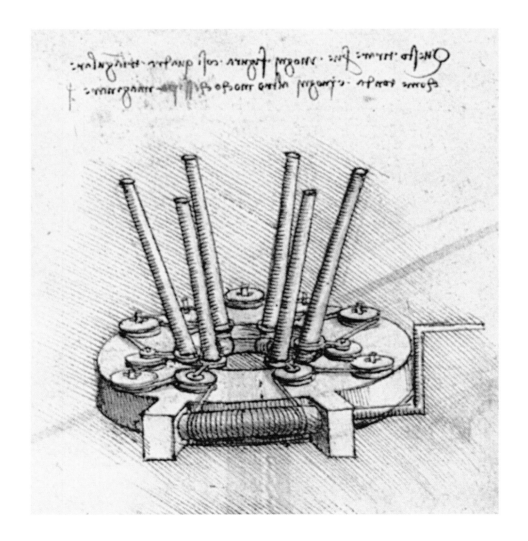

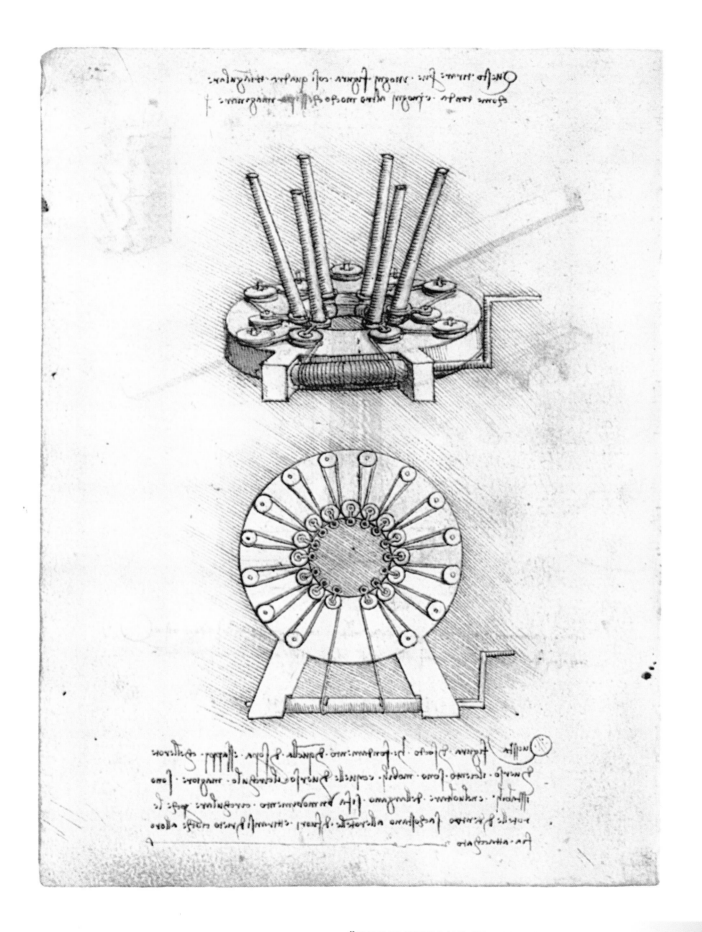

SPRING

c. 1497. Madrid Codex I, f. 85 r. Madrid, Biblioteca Nacional

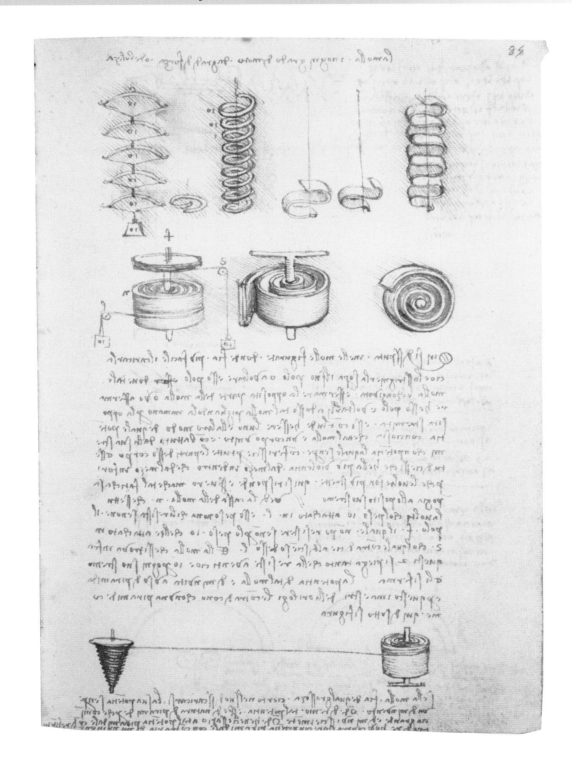

REMARKABLE IS the interest provided by Leonardo to the apparatuses with springs. That is already explicit since his juvenile years in his projects showing technical and scientific engagement, as his studies on the catapult (CA, ff. 140 *r-a*; b-*r*). The spring, together with the screw and the toothed wheel, will be one of the "mechanical elements", fundamental for the building and the functioning of his machines. For such reason it will be repeatedly and deeply examined with great attention in the Madrid Codex I (1492-95), the only book left of the four that would have had to consti-

tute his wide "*Trattato di meccanica*". Leonardo applied the spiral springs as a source of energy to the devices of clock-making as the toothed wheels; he devised also several gears of a spring engine (Madrid Codex I, ff. 4 *r*; 16 *r*; 45 *r*) and he even illustrated the production techniques, representing an appropriate machine to realize their different shapes (Madrid Codex I, f. 14 *v*): "Instrument to make a spring to give motion to a clock". Which thing was realized through the crushing of a metal bar, placed transversely, and with the help of a press, activated by a large screw with a crank.

BEARINGS WITH
THREE SPHERES

c. 1497. Madrid Codex I, f. 101 v. Madrid, Biblioteca Nacional

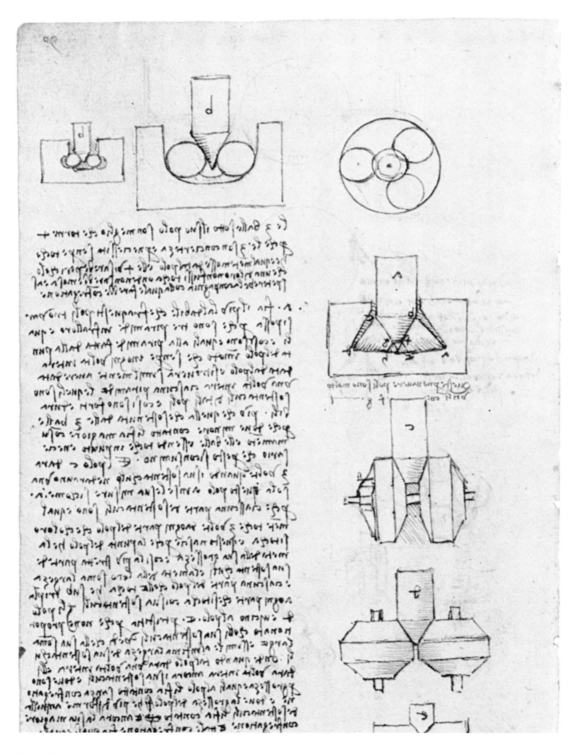

A SECOND arrangement of bearings, devised from Leonardo in order to reduce friction or to support the push of a vertical axle on which a burden is pressing, hypothesized the employment of three rolls or spheres that, arranged around the conical end of the axle could move freely in the hemispheric concavity that contained them. The artist-scientist emphasized its number rigorously, since the increase of a fourth sphere, altering the motion around the pivot, would have provoked more friction, failing thus its efficiency.

CLOCK

c. 1495-99. Madrid Codex, f. 27 v. Madrid, Biblioteca Nacional

LEONARDO WAS attracted by the measure of time since his juvenile years. Initially his approach was of a "qualitative and philosophical" type. Time, in coherence with the Pythagorean doctrine, described in Ovid's *Metamorphoses*, appeared to him to be "the one that consumes things" (CA, f. 195 *r*), other times he perceived its immeasurable vastness (Windsor, RL 19045 *v*), but he ended up to examine also its "quantitative" and mathematic aspects, in order to measure its scansion with greater precision and objectivity. The *recto* and *verso* of the sheet 1111 of the Codex Atlanticus, have revealed with how much interest he visited the Abbey of Chiaravalle, near Milan, to examine the operation of that famous weight-clock, placed in the tower, that not only recorded minutes and hours, but also the position of the Moon and of the Sun. But to improve the process of time measure, he devoted himself also to the study of the mechanisms of the clocks with springs, which were the technological innovation of Renaissance. In a variant of this type of clock, Leonardo adopted some gears connected by means of cables to a system of crossbow springs (CA, f. 863 r), which is a device quite similar to the one he employed for his "car" and that can be brought back perhaps to an escapement mechanism, used to regulate the release of the moving springs.

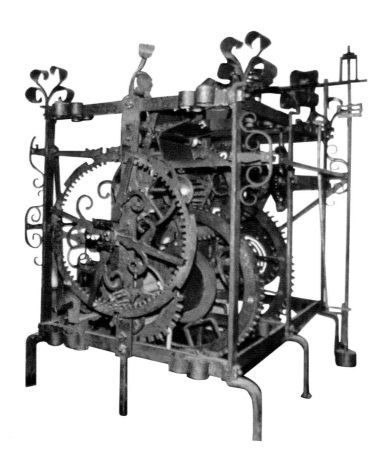

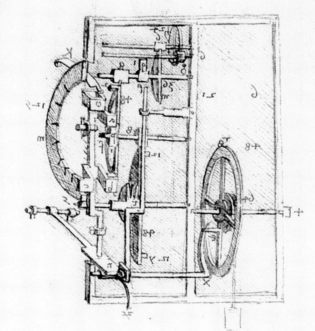

FLYWHEEL

c. 1497. Madrid Codex I, f. 114 r. Madrid, Biblioteca Nacional

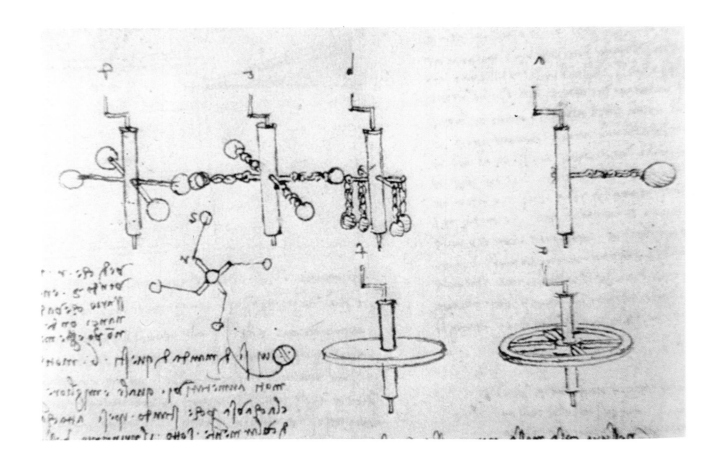

THE FLYWHEEL is a rotating organ of engines, used with the function of regulating their motion and the variations of speed. Leonardo was interested to its mechanism and, for its building, he designed two types of it, one with a wheel, with spokes joined to the hub of the vertical shaft, and the other, with vertical shaft, to which are joined, by means of chains, four weights or metallic spheres in state of quiet. In both projects the crank is put in the upper part of the shaft and with its spin, in virtue of the centrifugal force, the chains draw up with the spheres in horizontal position. To the speculation of Leonardo, this turns out to be a useful machine in the "augmentative motions", that is it becomes interesting after the overcoming of the starting point of inertia, when, after the spinning rate has been reached up, it follows a lessening of the effort and an easier conservation of motion.

STUDY OF
PERPETUAL MOTION

c. 1495-97. Madrid Codex I, f. 145 r. Madrid, Biblioteca Nacional

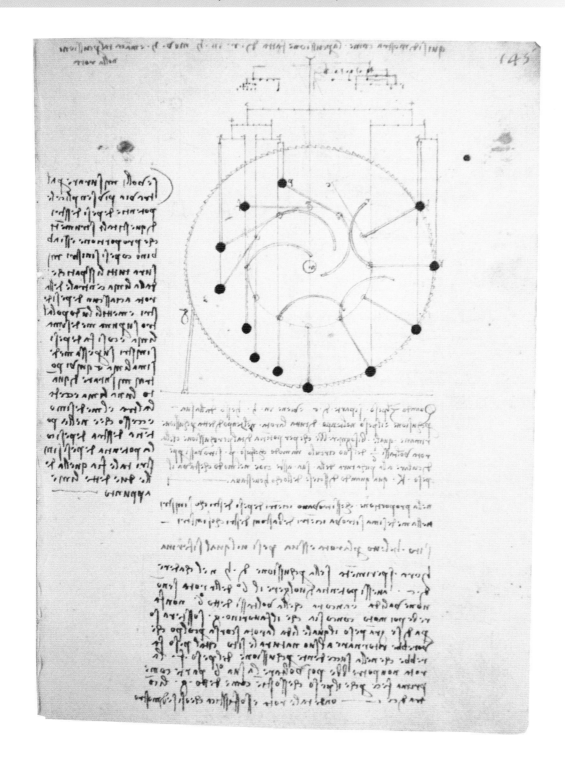

LEONARDO, IN controversy with the scientists of his time ("Speculators of continuous motion, how many varied engines in such search have you created! Do join the gold-seekers"), whose attitude he compares to that of the vain and deceptive speculations formulated by wizards and alchemists, attended to demonstrate on a theoretical plan the impossibility of perpetual motion, since no machine could have moved infinitely without receiving any energy from an external environment. Keeping to experience, Leonardo illustrates in this drawing a wheel, to the extremities of whose spokes are attached some weights, and to demonstrate it he writes in a note: "Whatever the weight that will be hung to the wheel, which weight is the cause of motion of that wheel, without any doubt the centre of such weight will stop under the centre of its pivot; and no instrument that can be manufactured by human talent and that turns round a pivot, will be able to escape such effect". Therefore every weight will stop under the center of its pole (or fixed point), reaching again its stable equilibrium, since the barycentre (or centre of gravity) is under the point of suspension and along its vertical. The same experiment is reproposed in Codex Foster II, ff. 90 v and 91 r.

THEATRICAL MACHINE FOR THE "ORPHEUS"

c. 1506-08. Private collection (from the f. 50 r. of the Codex Atlanticus)

RADICAL TECHNOLOGICAL innovations were produced by Leonardo also in the machines that he devised for his theatrical representations of the "*Paradiso*" by Bernardo Bellincioni (1490), on the occasion of the wedding in Milan of Giangaleazzo Sforza with Isabel of Aragon, and of the *Danae* by Baldassarre Taccone (1496), for the Count of Caiazzo, Gianfrancesco Sanseverino. The skill demonstrated in the construction of these machines with "special effects" and particularly impressive in the movements of descent and climbing, in which can be perceived an obvious derivation from Brunelleschi, made him famous at the court of Ludovico the Moor as a "preparer" of shows. But a technological innovation still more meaningful, and unprecedented in the history of theatre, can be recognized in the apparatuses that he managed to devise for the scenic preparation of the "*Orpheus*" by Poliziano in honour of Charles d'Amboise (Codex Arundel, ff. 231 *v* – 224 *r*), during his second stay in Milan. According to the drawings that we have, Leonardo, in his versatility as a director and as a mechanical engineer interested in motion, intended to represent the descent to Hades by Orpheus, dropping him in a naturalistic environment of steep and precipitous valleys and gorges. Then, opening wide a mountain through a system of gears, pulleys, pulling ropes and ball bearings, he made Pluto, King of the Underworld, appear on stage. He would have appeared transported from the depths of the earth by means of an ingenious elevator with a system of counterbalance, pulleys and traction ropes, ("When B lowers, A is raised and Pluto exits in H"; CA, f. 50 *r*), jumping suddenly into the middle of the uproar produced from the whimper of children and from the song of devils and of other infernal creatures, while a game of lights and shadows, skillfully produced, made the scene even more jerky and full of tension, in order to arouse in the audience a sense of wonder: "When the Paradise of Pluto opens, then here are devils playing twelve earthenware jars in the infernal way. Here is Death, the Furies, Cerberus, many naked infants crying; here are fires of several colou [rs...] in wine dancing".

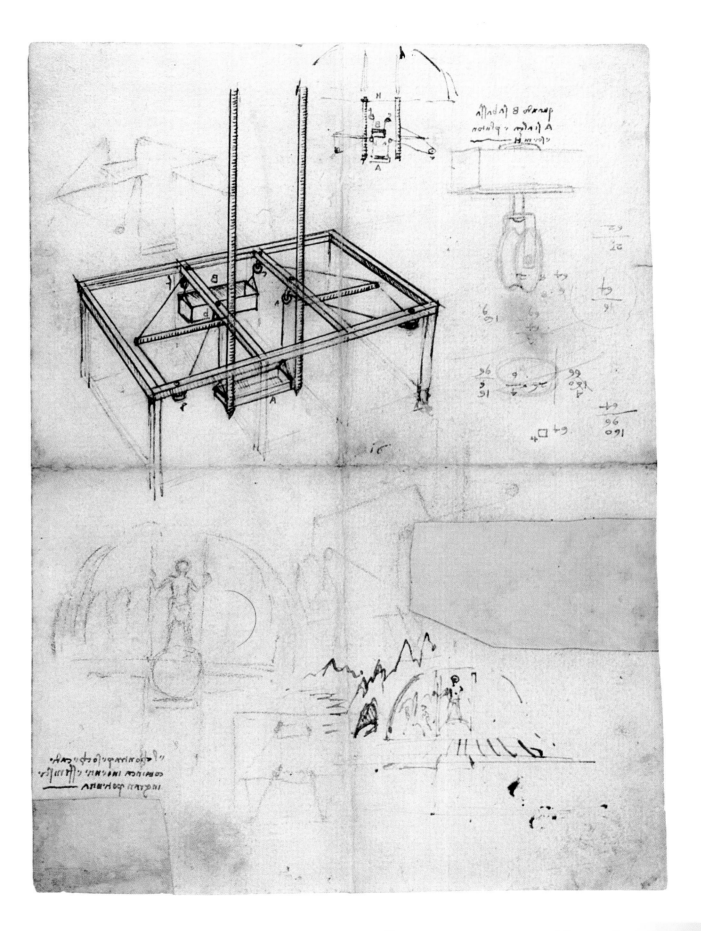

WATER MACHINES

SYSTEM
TO LIFT WATER

c. 1480. Codex Atlanticus, f. 1 bis r-a [5 r]. Milan, Biblioteca Ambrosiana

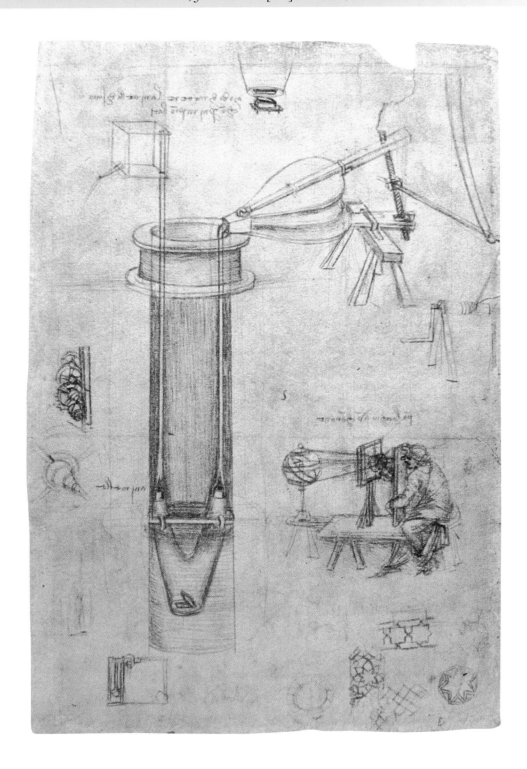

SINCE HIS formative years Leonardo was interested and occupied, like the engineers of his time and those that had preceded him, in the assiduous search of the several ways with which to lift water to various heights. In particular he was fascinated from the "screw of Archimedes", of which, knowing instinctively with innovative attitude its possible automation, he illustrated with a variety of formulas its construction and production (CA, f. 47 *r*), improving at the same time the devices already existing, once estimated the inclination of the spin axis and the number of turns. Beyond this hydraulic mechanism, Leonardo, on the outline of a cultural process transmitted from the Taccola and Francesco di Giorgio Martini, adopted other systems of hydraulic pumps, very defined on a technical and aesthetic level, and among these he made use of a great bellows machine, illustrated with great visual effectiveness also on folio 6 *r* of the Codex Atlanticus, which was able to lift water from the depth of a well with a circular section up into a tank, placed beyond the surface of the brickwork ring, after having created great air bubbles and having dipped them in the liquid, with the purpose of increasing its pressure.

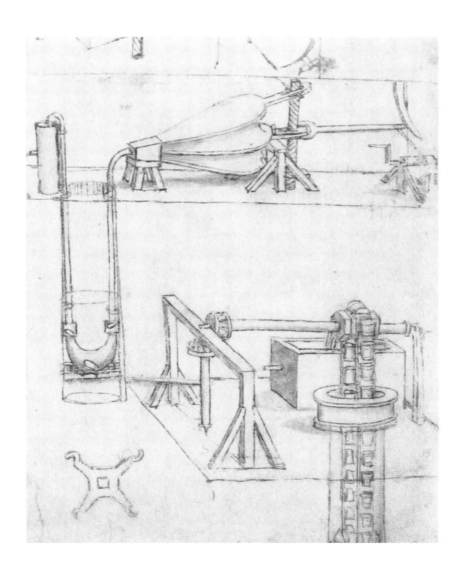

WAY TO WALK
ON THE WATER

c. 1480-82. Codex Atlanticus, f. 7 r-a [26 r]. Milan, Biblioteca Ambrosiana

IN THIS great sheet, also, dominated from the general topic of water, for the presence of hydraulic machines with related gears and wheels, it is present the plan, motivated from practical demands or war needs, of remaining underwater with the description of the head of a man equipped of glasses and a breathing apparatus ("cane", "cork", "way to go under water"). To this perspective it is associated, in the left medium section, a fast sketch of the way to walk on the water, where in the swift outline of the little human figure, who takes advantage of "leather bags" or wineskins, worn as if they were long shoes full of air, while he grasps two floating racquets in order to guarantee the orthostatic equilibrium of his person, Leonardo means to demonstrate how, for a sort of technological magic, the ancient human dream of walking on the surface of water can actually come true.

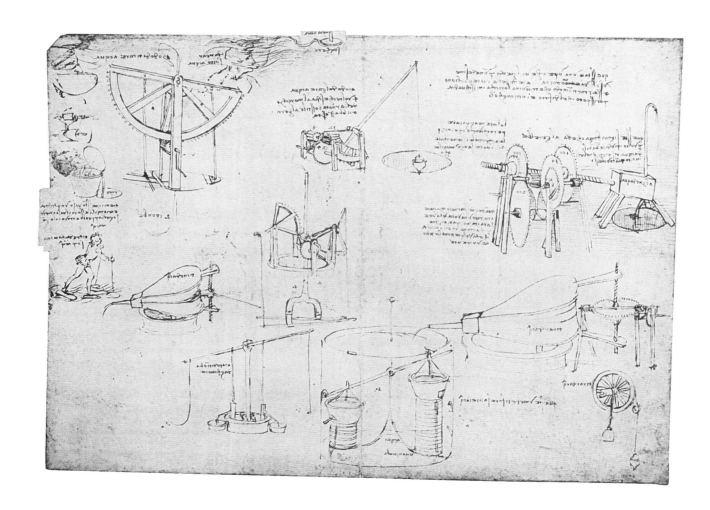

SCREW
OF ARCHIMEDES

c. 1480. Codex Atlanticus, f. 7 v-a [26 v]. Milan, Biblioteca Ambrosiana

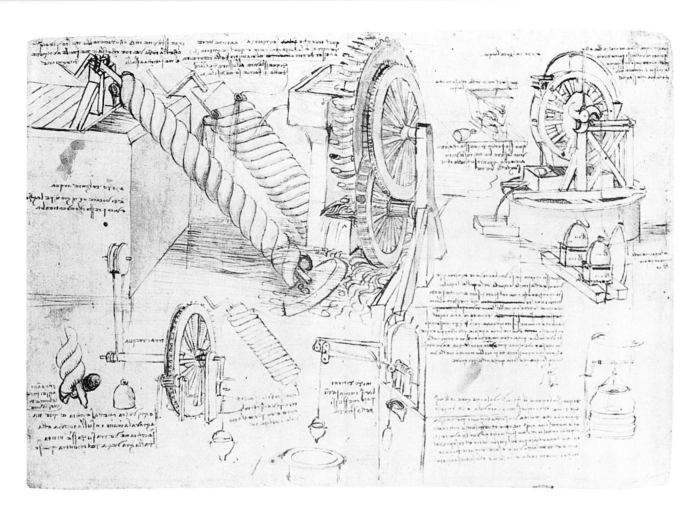

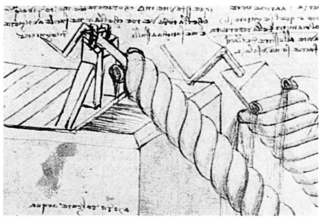

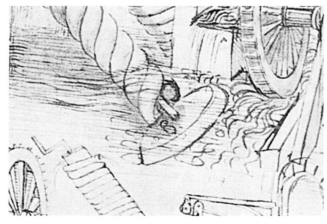

TO ARCHIMEDES (287-212 B. C.) it has been attributed not only the formulation of the laws of hydrostatics and the principle of the lever, but also the invention of instruments and machines like the burning glasses and the cochlea or Archimedean screw to lift water. Leonardo nourished an extraordinary veneration for the Greek scientist, that he considered the most brilliant inventor of antiquity and whose technical-scientific knowledge insistently tried to master. A short note of the Codex Atlanticus (f. 413 *r-v*) concerns to the *De Insidentibus in Humido*, where Archimedes exposed on a hydrostatic ground the problems of the floating bodies and of the bodies dipped in a fluid. The Codex of Madrid II (f. 112 *r*) contains another famous note, in which Leonardo thought he had squared the circle and at last he had overcome Archimedes in science. Besides, a contemporary of his, humanist Pomponio Gaurico, recognizing his high intellectual value had defined him, in 1504, as the most famous scholar endowed with "archimedaean genius". And the screw of Archimedes turned out to be to his mind, also for its singular spiral shape, a much admired mechanical element. Leonardo in fact was endlessly interested in extending and diversifying practically the field of its application to the sphere of hydraulics, where the cochleas, formed from tubes wrapped round to a rotating axis of a section mostly circular, through the rotatory motion given from a crank, favoured both the conveying of water from the depth of wells and its lifting, without any excessive human effort, from a low place up to great heights for the water supply of town centres (CA, f. 1069 *r*), let alone the draining of marshes. Giorgio Vasari loved to remember with emphasis that Leonardo mastered the science of waters, as he set up original solutions for works of hydraulic engineering, like "ways to drain harbours and trumpets to get low waters out of places".

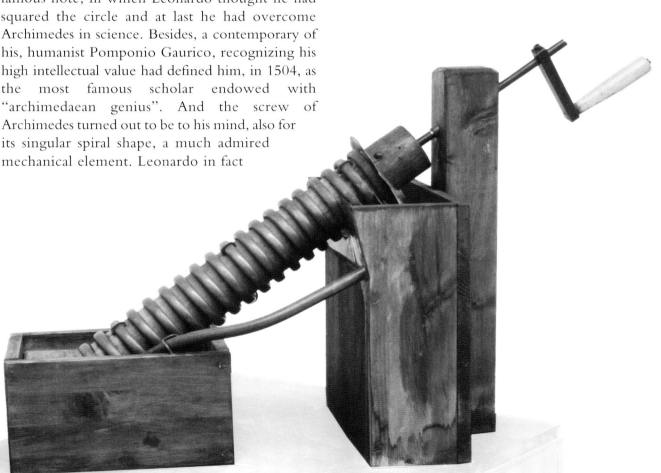

ARCHED BRIDGE

c. 1485-87. Codex Atlanticus, f. 22 r-a [69 a-r]. Milan, Biblioteca Ambrosiana

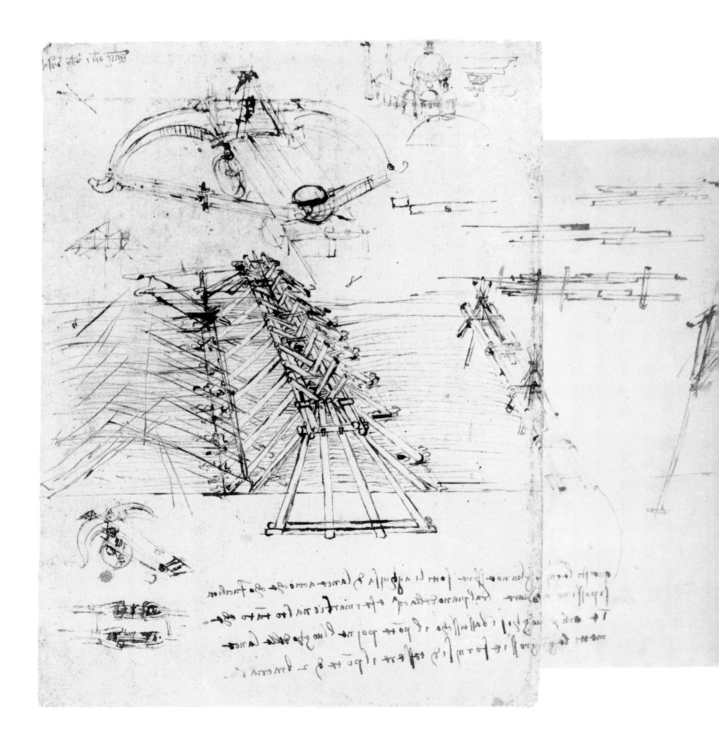

THE FIRST bridges to be built on occasion (CA, f. 55 *r*), devised from Leonardo and finalized to military aims, as they favoured the surprise factor and the fastest movements of troops and artilleries, were made of easily available materials like trunks and ropes, therefore substantially provisional and that could be quickly dismantled. In his letter to the Moor of 1483, the artist claimed his competent skill also in building "the lightest and strong" types of it. Besides, Luca Pacioli in person in his *De Viribus Quantitatis* would have remembered how Leonardo, being himself on the retinue of Cesare Borgia, had been inventor of improvised and ingenious makeshift bridges. But Leonardo had granted particular attention and interest also to the choice of the wooden material, holding in particular consideration the degree of its resistance: which was a sagacity deriving from his experience in the field of architecture (Codex B, ff. 15 *r*; 22 *v*), where the ribs, of small and great dimensions, had to support with their structure arches and vaults. The arched bridge, better known as "saving" bridge, as it guaranteed a way to escape and to find safety, was realized "not using other instruments, neither irons nor ropes", but only with joints, and it often revealed to be "sufficient and adequate to allow crossing" to an army.

MOBILE BRIDGE

c. 1487-89. Codex Atlanticus, f. 312 r-a [855 r]. Milan, Biblioteca Ambrosiana

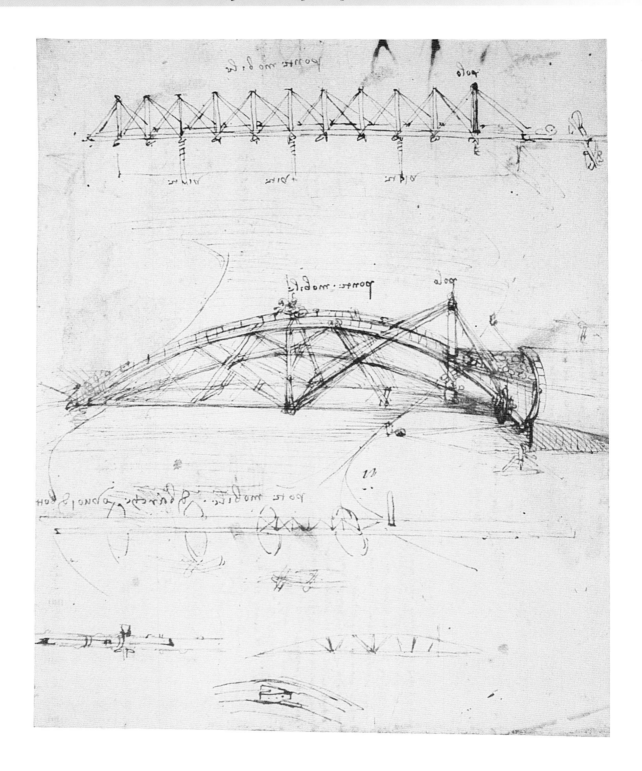

IN THE PLAN of the mobile bridge, always realized for war purposes, it is even more marked in Leonardo the extraordinary versatility in knowing how to correlate science, art and technology. The theoretical acquisition of the principles of the *De Ponderibus* passes now to a phase of experimental studies of statics and applied mechanics. The mobile bridge is made of a single span and is fixed to a bank with a vertical hinge or central pylon, around which it rotates. The movement takes place by means of ropes, winches for opening and closing, and with the aid of wheels and pulleys, which facilitate its sliding, while the counterbalance tank stabilizes its equilibrium and favours the manoeuvring, as soon as the bridge remains suspended, in order to allow passage to any possible boats.

HYDRAULIC SAW

c. 1478. Codex Atlanticus, f. 389 r-a [1078 a-r]. Milan, Biblioteca Ambrosiana

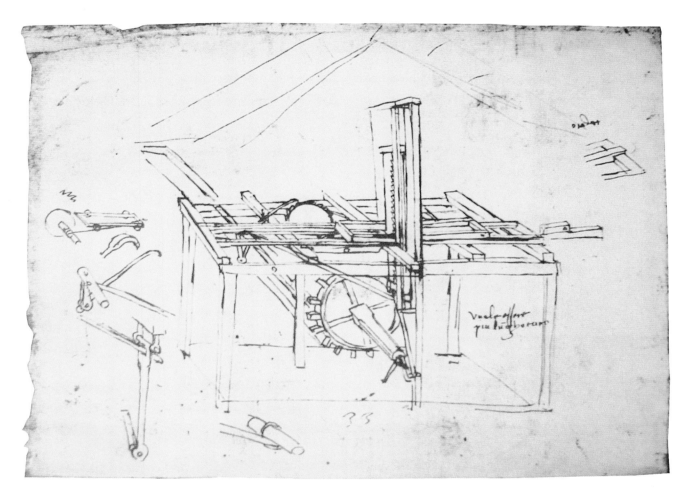

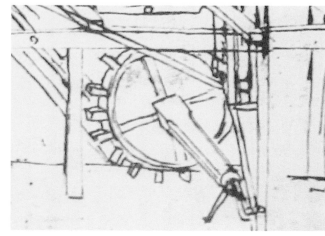

THIS HYDRAULIC machine is represented by Leonardo with a rapid sketch to pen and ink, which defines in part the chassis and the related mechanisms. The idea of the hydraulic machine has been probably copied from a model existing at his times and reveals how Leonardo still remains linked, at the beginning of the eighties, to the technological tradition of Tuscany, from which he wants to learn every type of information, before intervening with the necessary modifications to improve its working. In the machine, the wood trunk is transported horizontally from a trolley that advances gradually along rail tracks pulled from a rope winch, to be then cut from the saw that, placed inside the chassis, moves the blade in a vertical sense. Water, flowing in the underneath canal, determines the rotating motion of the hydraulic shovel wheel, which transfers mechanical energy and activates the various devices for the cutting of wood.

DIVER

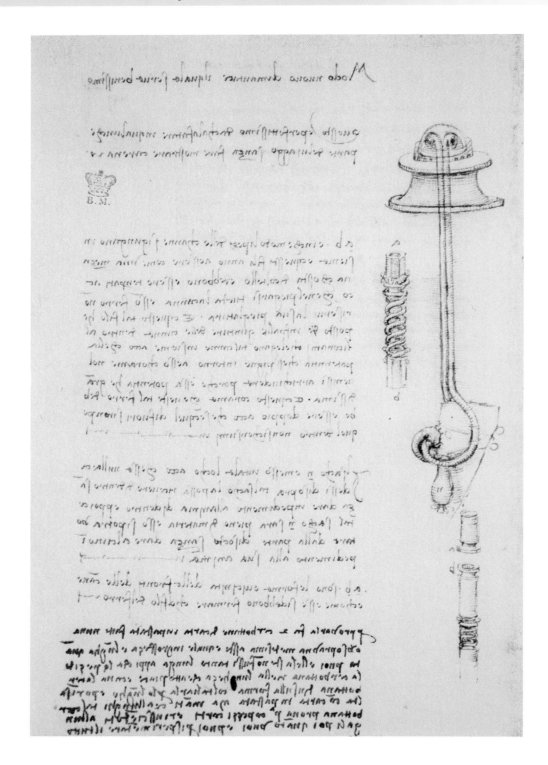

THE STUDY of Leonardo on the possible permanence of man under water did not constitute in itself an innovation, since already in medieval codices there had been illustrated its modalities, even if in quite a lot a rudimentary way, and the same contemporary engineers were experiencing it, like the great humanist and architect Leon Battista Alberti, that, in occasion of his attempt to recover the wrecks of the Roman ships laid down at the bottom of the lake of Nemi (1444), sent for a group of professional skin-divers from Genoa, paving the way to underwater archaeology. But nobody as Leonardo knew how to define and prefigure, with the analytic precision of his drawing and up to the smallest details, the modern solutions to prepare for that extraordinary enterprise. He in fact illustrates on several occasions with amazing originality the equipment and the indispensable devices for the underwater respiration of a diver (CA, f. 909 *v*), where the diving apparatus, realized in leather, had to be watertight, entrusting to a wide inflated chest bag and to a valve that regulated its air the possibility to come down or to carry out a fast surfacing, once gotten rid of the ballast. Moreover, the artist endows the diver with a respirator suitable to let him communicate with the external surface by means of flexible tubes, whose ending sector was protected from a floating cap. And while he was drawing the particulars of the valves for the entrance and the escape of the air, he was also carrying out physiology studies on lungs and respiration.

BOAT WITH DOUBLE HULL

c. 1484-86. Codex B, f. 11 r. Paris, Institut de France

LEONARDO WAS very fascinated from the idea of moving on the water or to descend under its surface for a long time. A challenge to the mysteries of nature, developed during the first years in which he was in Milan, when, inquiring on the existing tight correlation between air and water, the flight of birds and the swimming of man, he constructed flying machines and began studies of nautical engineering. Therefore he devised the realization of a boat with a watertight double hull ("Remember, before you enter and you close, to send breath out, so that it catches the amount of vacuum") and with a sharp prow, created to imitation of the shape of fishes and able to carry out immersions even in the abysses and the marine depths, and then able to go back to surface, protecting itself and minimizing any eventual effect of a break-through, provoked from enemy attacks. The plan of the submarine will be resumed by Leonardo in a sheet of the

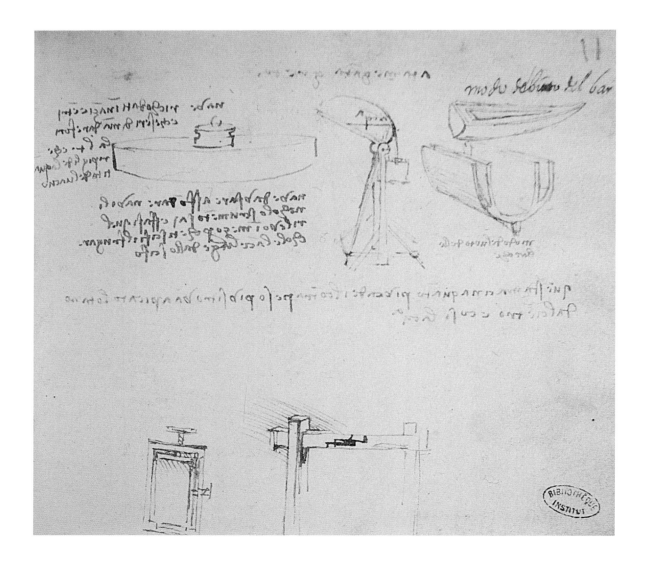

Codex Atlanticus (f. 881 *r)*, where it will be equipped of oars and fins to advance under water and of one sail to move on the surface of water. To this system of war with foresight sceneries approaches also the invention of the keel–breaker (CA f. 909 *v)*, of which the diver could have taken advantage in his submarine incursions to disembowel the planking of the enemy ships. It will be under this circumstance that Leonardo will motivate the secrecy of his studies on staying under water, securing himself from the enslavement of his own inventions to the lust of those who would only take advantage of them to provoke death and destruction ("and this I do not publish nor divulge for the bad natures of men, who would use the assassinations in the bottom of the seas"). It was so opened, ahead of three centuries in respect of the "Nautilus" of Robert Fulton (1798), the submarine age. In fact, Cesare Cesariano, in the years in which Leonardo compiled the CodexHammer (1506-13), would have planned a vessel with which he could navigate under water, from the moats of the Sforza Castle in Milan up to the Castle of Musso, on the lake of Como.

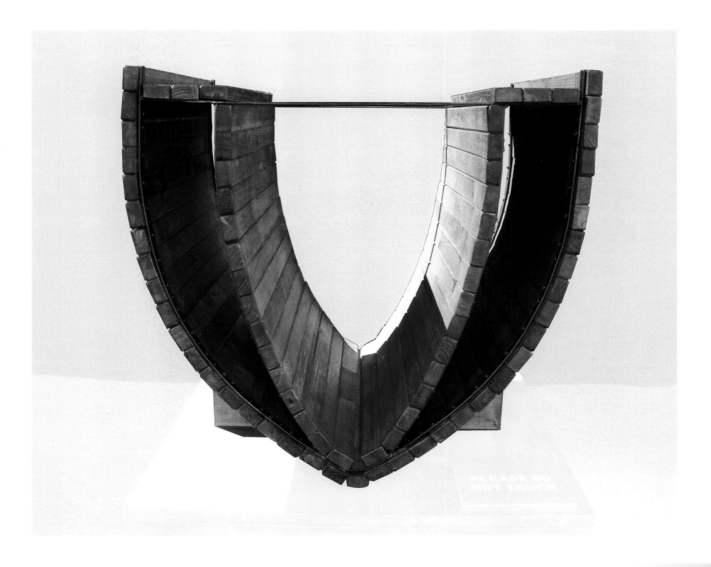

BOAT WITH
SHOVELS

c. 1484-86. Codex B, f. 83 r. Paris, Institut de France

IN THE FIRST years of his career as an engineer, Leonardo carries on also researches in order to make navigation quicker on the slow waters of canals, lakes and rivers, perceiving its great usefulness and advantages for the mercantile and military activities. Therefore, planning a new type of boat, he devoted himself to studies on the floatation of boats with further appraisals of static and dynamic nature, equalizing their hull to the shape of the fishes and adopting a new system of propulsion with the use of great rotating shovels, suitable to increase with a lesser waste of energies the movement speed. The shovels, equipped of a complex and effective system of gears, were intended to replace the traditional use of oars and sails. A sailor, placed under the deck of the ship, pushing with force on pedals or making use of a system of handle-bars, would have transmitted energy to the central sprocket wheel and from here to the shovels. This navigation system would have earned a large consent in America, above all in the nineteenth century along the Mississippi, where the famous boats equipped with great wheels became the most suitable ones for the transportation of passengers and light cargos.

LIFE JACKET

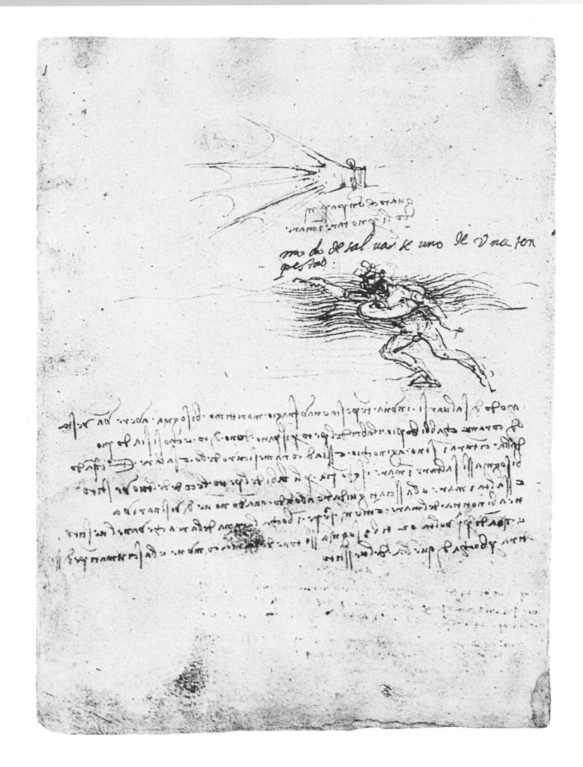

THE CARE reserved by the artist-engineers of the fifteenth century to the graphic representation of their machines and to the various inventions they carried out appeared to be the will of an intellectual expression subtended to reaffirm the value of mechanical arts over "humanae litterae". Therefore Leonardo, though aware of facing subjects already considered by a philosophical-scientific tradition, that from Ruggero Bacone (*Epistola de Secretis Operibus Artis et Naturae*) reaches Mariano di Jacopo called the Taccola (*De Ingeneis*), he lingers in the same sheet to think about and to investigate on how to improve further the swimming capacities of man. The first technological and scientific interest, as far as the principle of Archimedes is involved, is reserved to the webbed glove or "glove with membranes to swim in the sea", destined to improve the floatation of man in water and to do so that the movements of the arms might allow a greater push in every direction. Leonardo, continuously pushed to search analogies in the components of the natural world, takes the limb of the web-footed animals as his model and hypothesizes a glove to tie around the wrist, made up of five sticks, like an extension of fingers, and of one membrane. In the underlying part, Leonardo draws a human figure to which, beyond making a complete spin of the bust in order to suggest the action of swimming in free style, he makes wear a life jacket, suggesting taking advantage of it in case of storm or tempest: "way to escape in a storm and marine shipwreck". Furthermore, even in notes of technical and military strategy, Roberto Valturio (1405-75), in his *De Re Militari* and Francesco di Giorgio Martini (1439-1501), in his *Opusculum De Architectura*, had illustrated the method to overcome the currents of a river, equipping the army of "leather bags" full of air.

DREDGE

c. 1513-14. Codex E, f. 75 v. Parigi, Institut de France

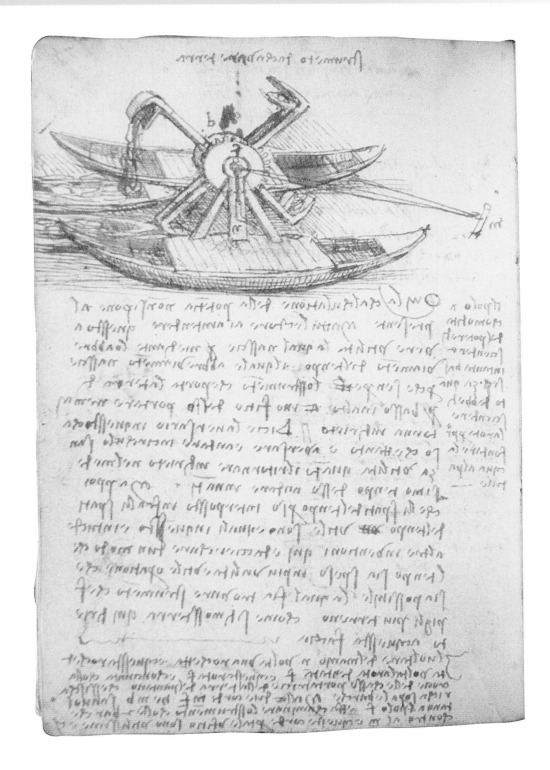

THE DREDGE, or mud-extractor, made of two boats with the shape of a raft, whose hulls are so tightly fixed in their transversal sense by the structure of a large wheel with spoons, sends back with visual inmediacy, due to its shape and its singular stability in floatation, to the configuration and the equilibrium reached with the most modern catamarans. A small barge, placed inside, carried out the function of collecting mud, removed by the spin of the shovels from the bed of a river or the bottom of a swamp. The operation of the dredge took place through a crank placed on the axis of the wheel, which, wrapping a rope, anchored on the bank, around the drum, adjustable in vertical sense to diversify the depth of the operations of cleaning and of excavation, allowed its operating advance or its recovery to unload the accumulated material. This invention was probably used by Leonardo when, around 1515, he received the assignment from Giuliano de' Medici, brother of Pope Leone X, as "most skilful geometrician" and hydraulic engineer, to supply the reclaiming of the Pontine Marshes, in the south of Rome between the Circeo and Terracina (Windsor, RL 12684 *r*). In putting into effect a plan of integral drainage, Leonardo would have taken advantage not only of this machine for the water-drainage of the channels, but also of a system of pumps, expressly devised in order to empty swamps and lake basins (Codex F, f. 15 *r*).

MACHINES
FOR THE FLIGHT

BRUSH AND FUNNEL ANEMOMETERS

c. 1487-90. Codex Atlanticus, f. 249 v-a, b [675 r]. Milan, Biblioteca Ambrosiana; *Codex Arundel, f. 241 r.* London, British Library

IN THE DEVELOPMENT of his searches on the flight, Leonardo examined also the motion of the air and of the wind, knowing instinctively that his flying machine interacted with them, considered that the aerial currents and the "continuous percussions" of the last one were capable to provoke a variation in their trajectories, speed and height. Therefore, availing himself of a technology derived from the experience of the "mechanical arts", he devised also the anemometer, that is to say an apparatus that served to measure the speed of the wind, in order to take advantage of it in some of his experiments. He designed two different types of this device, a simpler one, called "with foils" or "with brush", and constructed in a not particularly careful style, the other one more elaborated and complex, called "with funnel". In the first case, the device is an apparatus in graduated wood with a metal foil, which is shifted according to the intensity and the direction of the wind. In the second case (Codex Arundel, f. 241 *r*), the device aims to verify if the pressure of the wind that sets in action the motion of a rotor or bladed wheel is proportional to the opening of the cones, through which pass the flows of the fluid. Today, the anemometers are installed in the most modern airplanes, in order to measure the static and dynamic pressure that is created with the motion of the airplane itself through the air, and which changes with varying of speed.

STUDY OF A UNITED WING

c. 1480. Codex Atlanticus, f. 313 r-b [858 r]. Milan, Biblioteca Ambrosiana

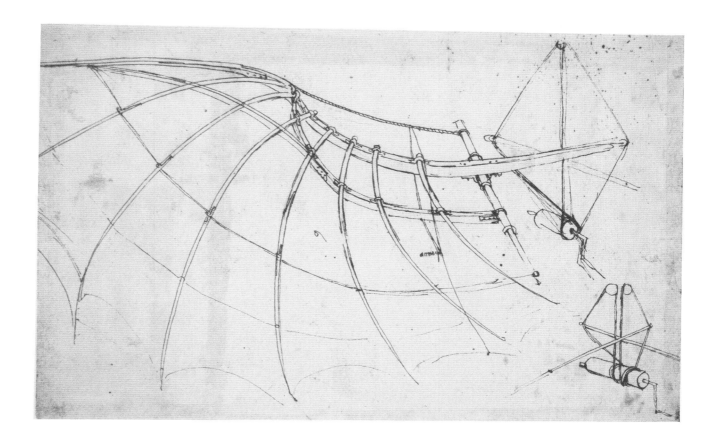

IN HIS STUDY on the flight, Leonardo initially shows a great confidence in the infinite dynamic possibilities of man, being convinced of the tightened anatomical and functional interrelation between man and the birds. Therefore, after having studied a kind of wing with "doors" (CA, ff. 74 *r*, 309 *v-b*), in other words a wing with mobile openings that could be closed and reopened, developed on the supposition that at the moment of taking wing the feathers are widened in order to let the air pass and then they are closed tightly in order to exercise a greater pressure on the fluid, he devised, following the mimetic principle of nature and imitating therefore the shape of the wings of bats, this new kind of a "united" wing. This type of flapping wing presumed the use of one and only "cloth" laying on a framework composed of a very light material made of wood and canes, entrusting to a crank, moved from the man placed at the centre of a small ship, the function of moving the wings, by winding the pulling rope on a roll. Such a mechanism on the other side let us suppose that the "united" wing, substantially devoid of any organic technical connotations of a machine, was not destined to the experimentation of human flight, but was aimed to reproduce the flight of angels or demons in the theatrical animations in religious or profane shows, that were staged in Florence since the time of the great architect Filippo Brunelleschi, like the famous representation of the Ascension.

GLIDER

c. 1493-95. Codex Atlanticus, f. 309 v-a [846 v]. Milan, Biblioteca Ambrosiana

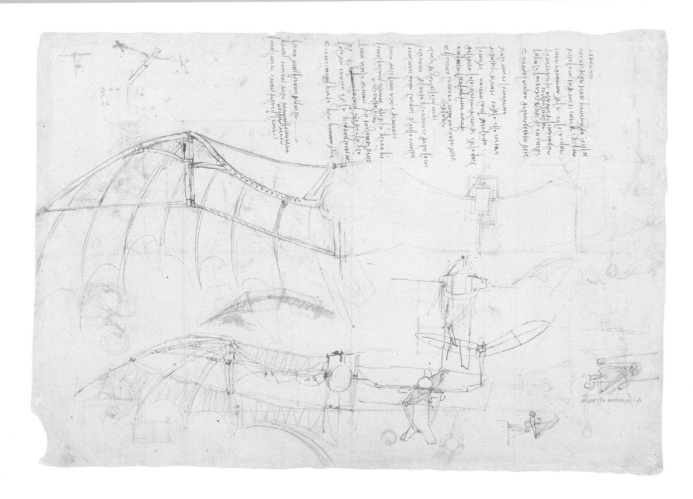

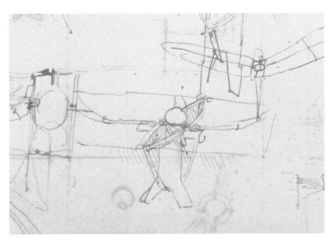

AT THE BEGINNING of the Nineties of the fifteenth century, Leonardo, with reference to his researches conducted on the mechanical flight, abandons the study of the flight with a flapping wing, in order to experience the one with a partially fixed wing. The conception of this machine, commonly defined ornithopter, undoubtedly constitutes a progress in aerodynamic research, though it turns out to be still inadequate for sustentation in flight and still founded on the search for a technology that multiplies the force of man. In fact, it proposes itself like an intermediate experience aimed to reach the typology of the glider, where man will succeed in directing the machine, making use with skill of the movements of his body for the equilibrium and the change of direction. The complicated systems and the gears imagined to transmit the necessary motion to the flap of wings, become simpler. The wing as a whole is no more composed of a structure one and only, but it is broken and conceived as partially fixed. The wing remains fixed and rigid in the inner sector nearer to the pilot, who, master of the machine and of the air (in the mind of Leonardo at least), finds his place, supported from a sling of straps, at the centre (in a strongly anthropocentric vision) also in a vertical sense in order to guarantee with just his weight the balance of the structure, to which he is directly connected, while the extreme part of the wing is now mobile, with the aim to govern the direction of the apparatus, by manoeuveuring handles, ropes and pulleys.

FLYING
MACHINE

c. 1485-87. Codex Atlanticus, f. 302 v-a [824 v]. Milan, Biblioteca Ambrosiana

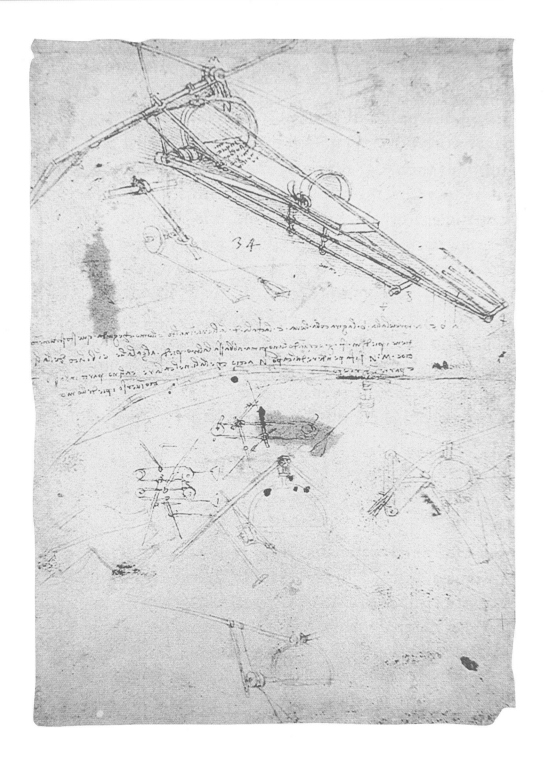

THIS VERY defined drawing on the human flight, repeated in the Codex B (f. 74 *v*), is one of the most famous, since it describes still on the project ground the structure of the flying machine, complete of wings and pilot, who is placed in a prone position on the platform ("in this place comes the core") and kept busy on a dynamic plan developing and taking advantage of all the parts of the body for the propulsion of the device. The image is accompanied with very important notes, since they explain the operations of the complex mechanisms leading the composite movement of the wings, activated from the pilot who is pushing with his feet on the pedals F and G, so that the one raises and the other closes the wing: "A twists the wing, B turns it with the lever, C lowers it, D lifts it up". These are precise indications of manoeuvre of the three pairs of ropes that, in grace of a system of pulleys, fold the extremity of the wing in order to open it and to close it, bend it and make it perform by means of a lever a rotating movement.

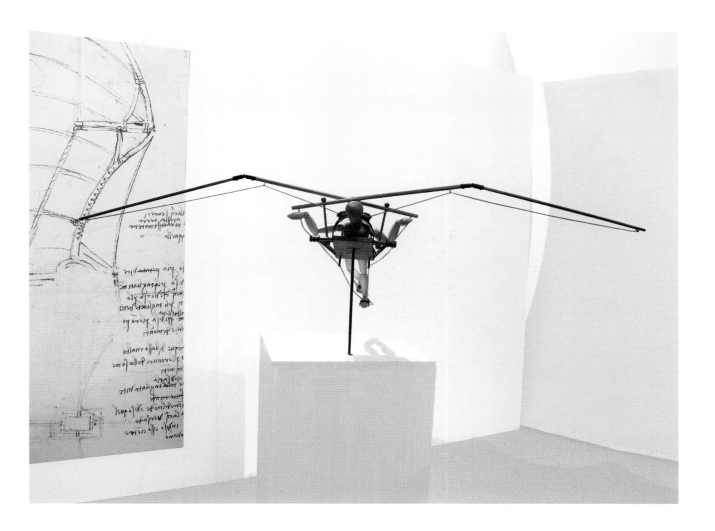

CLINOMETER

c. 1485. Codex Atlanticus, f. 381 r-a [1058 r]. Milan, Biblioteca Ambrosiana

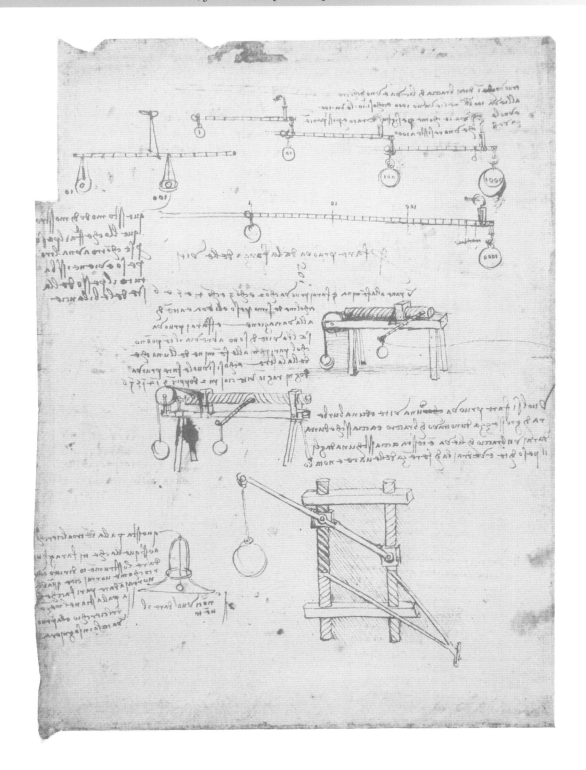

THE CLINOMETER is an onboard flight instrument employed like a plumb-line during the flight operations and it is used to measure the verticality, that is to say it allows the pilot to maintain the proper equilibrium and the necessary inclination for the correct guide of the flying machine during the operations carried out to turn around the vertical axis. It is made of a pendulum, placed within a glass bell, so as not to endure alterations provoked from wind blasts: "It is necessary that the wind does not blow on it. This ball within the circle is the one that will make you guide the device straight or twisted, as you will want, that is when you want to go even, let the ball in the middle of the circle, and the test will teach you". Leonardo, planning the ornithopter with bicycle (CA, f. 897 r), equipped it with this instrument, putting it over the head of the pilot.

PARACHUTE

c. 1485. Codex Atlanticus, f. 381 v-a [1058 v]. Milan, Biblioteca Ambrosiana

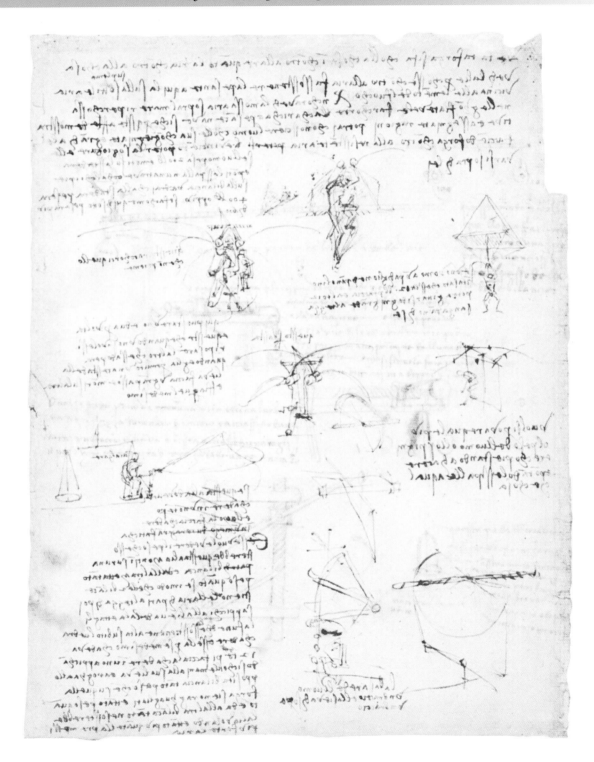

MACHINES FOR THE FLIGHT

LEONARDO, THAT as artist-engineer was on the same experimental line traced from the "mechanical" tradition of Tuscany, "invented" also the parachute ("a pavilion of airproof linen cloth"), that, even if present in the drawings of an anonymous engineer of Siena of the fifteenth century (Codex Add. 34113, ff. 189 *v* and 200 *v*, London, British Library), he then led back and folded to his experiences of flight "without a flap of wing". After having carried out studies of aerostatics and of aerodynamics, he sensed by intuition that man, availing himself of a parachute of remarkable dimensions ("that is 12 arms for face and high 12") and therefore able to exercise a strong pressure on the air and to meet a significant resistance, would have received an adequate deceleration in his descent and would have avoided a ruinous impact to the ground, even throwing himself from a remarkable height: "He will be able to throw himself from great height without damage for him".

VERTICAL
ORNITHOPTER

c. 1488-89. Codex B, f. 80 r. Paris, Institut de France

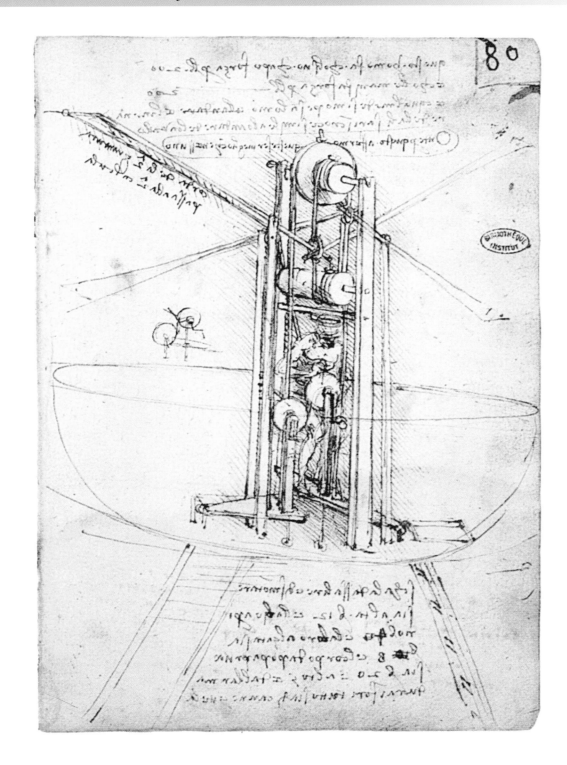

IN THE THEORETICAL attempt to develop to the maximum the necessary force to impart energy to the shovels of this extraordinary flying machine, Leonardo keeps all the parts of the human body busy. So he places the pilot in erected station and he compels him, being at the centre of the small ship, to activate a complex mechanism of ups and downs for the transmission of the alternate motion, not only with arms and legs, but also with the head ("this man pushes with his head for 200 pounds and with his hands he pushes for 200 pounds; and which is the same the man weights [...] whence and for this I affirm that it is better than any thing else"). The machine is structured like a boat vessel of enormous dimensions. The small ship of circular shape has a length of 12 meters, equivalent to the ladders of connection between the earth and the cockpit, which have to be long to take off best ("look at the swift that if he is put on earth he cannot take wing, because he has short legs"). The wing span turns out to be of 24 meters with amplitude of stroke of 4,8 meters. Considered the remarkable dimensions of the machine, Leonardo thought that it was necessary the presence of four wings, distributed in pairs and supplied of a movement that, for the sustension and the moving forward of the machine, struck "in cross, similar to the advancing of a horse". At the same time, Leonardo adopted for the vertical ornithopter a system of takeoff and landing (Codex B, f. 89 *r*), taking a meticulous care over the retractable ladders, which he wanted to equip with particular shock-absorbers, in order to make the landing softer: "These hooks that are made under the bottom of the ladder, they do the same office of that one who jumps down on tiptoe, that he does not stun his person, as if he jumped on the heels".

AERIAL SCREW

AMONG THE most renowned drawings of mechanical utopia concerning flight, there is the famous device of the "aerial screw", interpreted like an anticipation of modern helicopters. Leonardo in the note underneath the plan writes: "I think, if this instrument in form of a screw will be made well, that is, it will be made of linen cloth, stopped its pores with starch, and turned with ability, that the aforesaid screw will be female in the air and it will climb up". The screw, covered of linen and with a radius of 4,8 meters, would have had to rise in air, considered as a compressible fluid if submitted to a certain pressure, and would havev had to penetrate in it quickly like usually a screw does in other materials. The spin, which would have imparted a push upward to the machine, would have been achieved with physical force, quickly unrolling a rope under the axis or by means of horizontal levers, implanted on the central shaft and pushed from a group of men running around it.

FLAPPING WING

c. 1487-90. Codex B, f. 88 v. Paris, Institut de France

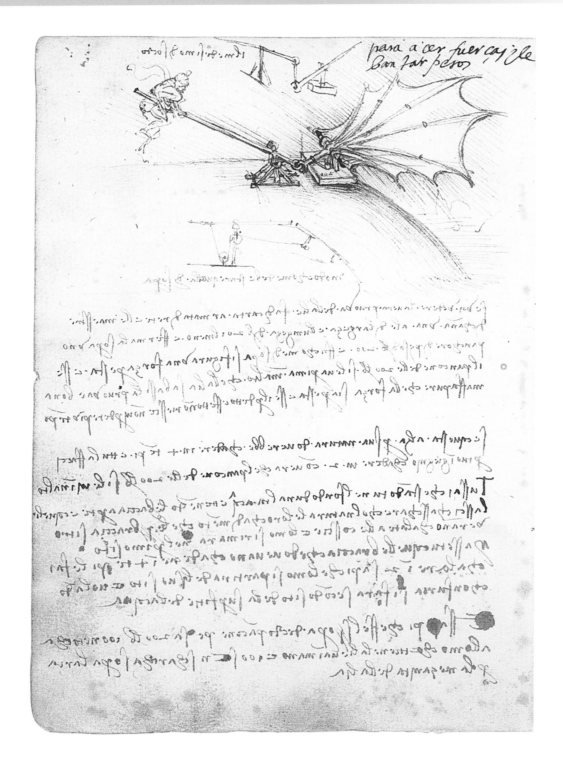

IN LEONARDO, human flight is not a simple literary quotation, that it sends back to the myth of Icarus, because he truly believes that it is feasible, by repeating the mechanisms with which the world of nature is structured. Therefore, in the challenge of natural laws, when he planned a flying machine, he initially attended to the realization of flight with a flapping wing following considerations of statics (laws of the weights and of gravity) and of dynamics. Therefore he wanted to verify experimentally if the push of the artificial wing, moved fast, could support the body of man in his flight. To such purpose, in the caption underneath the drawing, explaining the connected dynamic implications, the artist commented: "If you want to see the true test of the wing, make a wing of paper, armed with net and the masters of canes, of 20 arms of width and length, and stopped over one bench of 200 pounds of weight; and give it,

like above is depicted, a strong force. And if the bench of 200 pounds rises up before the wing is lowered, the test is good; but let the force given be strong, and if the foretold effect does not succeed, do not lose your time in it". Leonardo wanted to put to test his plan on the top of a high hill, using a "bench" of approximately 68 kilos, on which to fix the great mechanical wing, with its chassis made of canes and a panniculus of paper covered of net. It was wide approximately 12 meters and, with its flap, made possible by an adequate force quickly and repeatedly exercised on the lever from a man, it would have had to raise that weight. Leonardo considered that, only appealing to the force and speed of the human push, the air under the wing would have been subject to pressure downwards, determining that equal and contrary push of the mass upwards, that would have allowed it sustentation during the flight.

HANG-GLIDER

c. 1495. Madrid Codex 1, f. 64 r. Madrid, Biblioteca Nacional

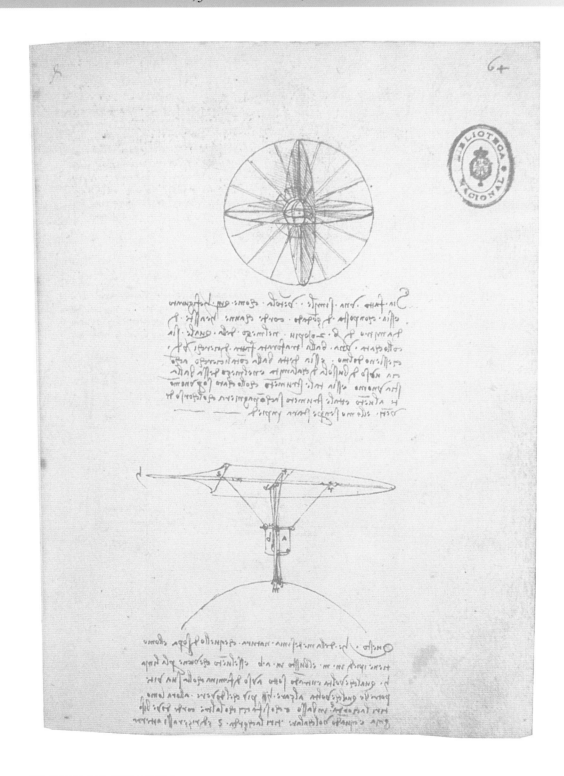

AT THE MIDDLE of the nineties, during his first Milan stay, the alternative plan of a flying machine pushes his way through in Leonardo. After having put aside the beating flight based on a man that actively puts in action a system of levers and pulleys in order to lower and to raise the wings, to realize the dream of flight, the only possibility is to entrust gliding and aerostatic flight, which means to use the wind like engine of the whole. It will be an absolutely new experience, in which the pilot will have to make use and to avail himself not only of brute force, but also of talent and skill, in order to reach the equilibrium and to exploit the direction of the wind like in a glider. Leonardo, designing two extraordinary devices for sailplaning, which take advantage of a deformable or cardanic

mechanical joint and entrust themselves to the course of the winds, puts the man in an erected position in the first, inside a spherical and perforated cockpit at the centre of an impeller circular machine ("And such instrument has to be placed over a mountain, to the wind, and such instrument will follow the course of the winds, and the man will always stand"), and in the other puts him in a horizontal position, under a machine which has a longitudinal shape, similar to a great kite, controllable from ground by means of cables. Both these flight systems make use of sails and preannounce the affirmation in the skies of the present hang-glider: "With this conclusion, it is deduced that the weight of man can, by means of a great width of wing, be sustained through the air" (Codex E, f. 39 *r*).

MILITARY
MACHINES

CIRCUMFOLGORE

c. 1503-05. Codex Atlanticus, f. 1 r-b [1 a-r]. Milan, Biblioteca Ambrosiana

THIS EXTRAORDINARY war machine, illustrated with the finest hatching and the splendour of the water-coloured drawing, it is expression of the titanic creativity of Leonardo, always ready to devise and to submit to the attention of some illustrious gentleman or commander his inventions or his war machines, whose devastating effects would have imposed the adoption of new military strategies. As he had already done with the naval gun that fired incendiary projectiles (Windsor, RL 12652), once again, Leonardo thinks to equip a boat, that works on the open sea and that moves in this case with shovel wheels, with an armament both fast and lethal in order to offend an enemy fleet. The circumfulgore or multiple bombard was a system of rotatory artillery equipped of sixteen guns disposed on one platform and it was capable of giving off an enormous firepower.

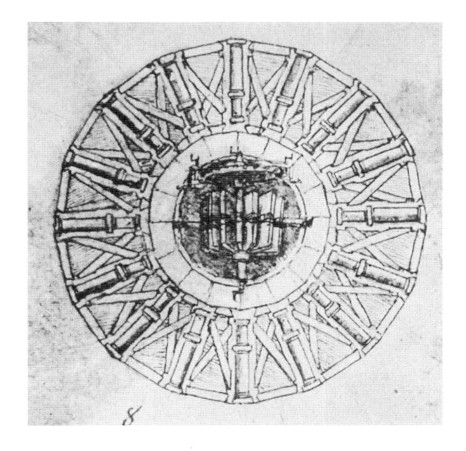

BOMBARD

c. 1485. Codex Atlanticus, f. 9 v-a [33 r]. Milan, Biblioteca Ambrosiana

THE REPRESENTATION of the mechanical structure of mortars and of the effects produced from the explosive balls punctually seems to answer and to be connected to a precise technical and military program with which Leonardo intends to gain credit before Ludovico the Moor. Exactly in the fourth and in the eighth paragraph of his famous letter sent to the Duke, around 1483, with the purpose to provoke astonishment, interest and favourable appreciations for his future services, he writes: "I still have many of bombards the most comfortable and easy to carry, and with which to throw tiny stones with resemblance to a storm, and with the smoke of that able to give great fright to the enemy, with serious damage for him and confusion", and later on: "As

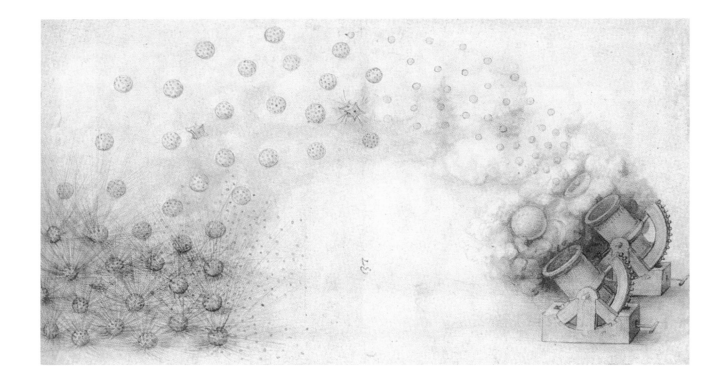

well, being necessary, I will make bombards, mortars and long-range culverins of the most beautiful and useful shapes, out of the common use". The innovation of this war project rose up in the mind of Leonardo from the reflections on the various ways to use the artilleries, now against the bastions of fortresses and now against an army in motion and in an open field, sometimes lined up on many fronts. If the large and heaviest iron balls shot from these bombards, with a stocky and short barrel and mounted on a sturdy support, could produce destructive effects towards a motionless target, having a tracking system that allowed regulating the degrees of shooting and the trajectory of launch, little damage in truth they caused to infantry soldiers and knights. Therefore Leonardo turns to the invention of the "ballots", which explode with a spectacular display of powder and smoke from the fire mouth of the mortars (Codex A, f. 111 r, c. 1492), with an artistic rendering of great evocative force and attentive scientific control, in relation too to their parabolic path. At the very moment of their impact with the ground, from their holes comes out in every direction a number of fragmentation projectiles with deadly effects in their range of action, anticipating in an amazing way the most modern war machines.

DEFENCE
OF WALLS

c. 1482-85. Codex Atlanticus, f. 49 v-b [139 r]. Milan, Biblioteca Ambrosiana

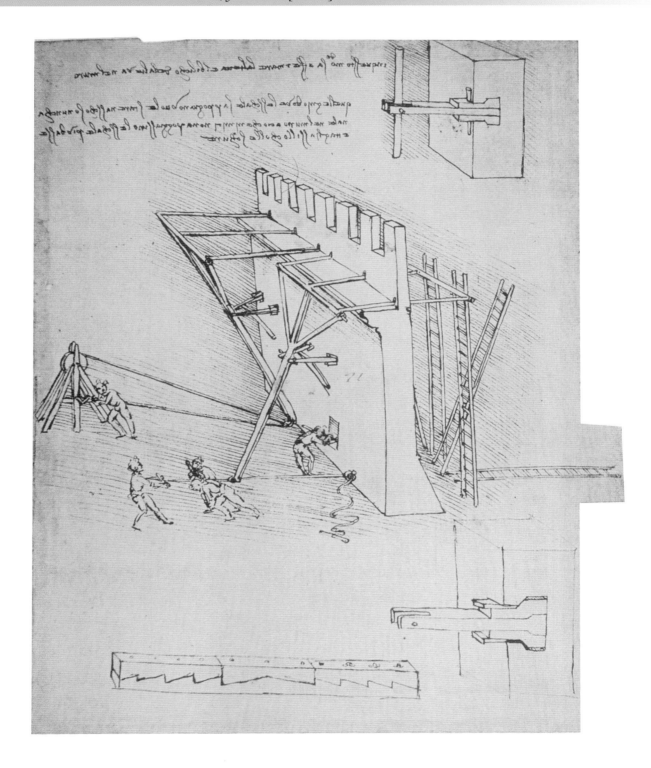

LEONARDO DEVISED a series of exemplary projects for the defence of walls from enemy onslaught, showing clearly how much importance he credited to practical knowledge. The drawing here examined proves all his familiarity with the great "mechanical" tradition of Tuscany (Brunelleschi, Verrocchio, Mariano di Jacopo said the Taccola, Francesco di Giorgio Martini), where art, science and technique lived in a kind of symbiosis, in order to concur to a definition on the visual ground of the structure and functionality of a machine. The devised defensive system, made contextual, reveals all its effectiveness in rejecting an onslaught of enemies, based on the use of ladders in order to exceed the town-walls. A long beam hidden and embedded in the high part of the walls, between the communication trench and the battlement ("so that the enemies could not lean further down their ladders and could not cut it with their axes"), would have emerged with force overturning the ladders of the besiegers, following a manoeuvre carried out from the inside by many of men, that visibly animated and in motion set in action a system of levers, winches and pulling ropes.

CATAPULT

c. 1485-90. Codex Atlanticus, ff. 50 v-a, v-b [140 a-r, b-r]. Milan, Biblioteca Ambrosiana

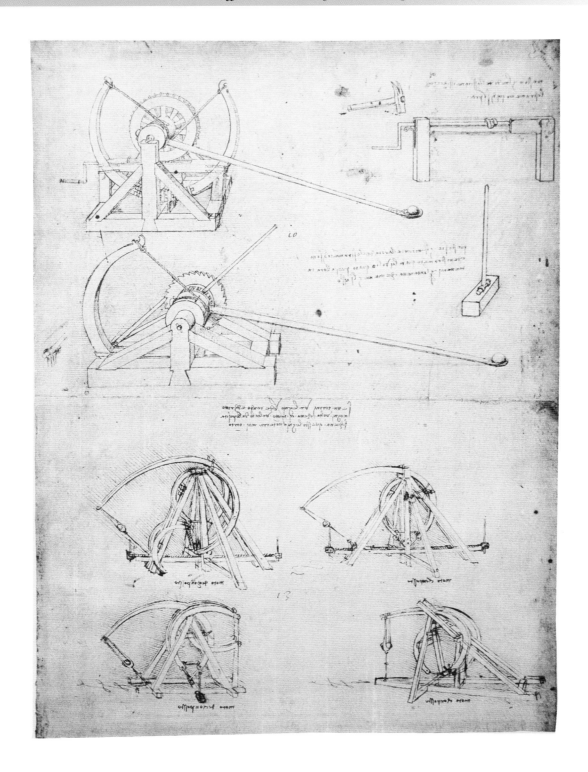

AMONG THE war machines that since his youth fascinated the fantasy and the creativity of Leonardo, there was the catapult. Commonly known and used since antiquity in battles or in besieges, at the times of Leonardo it had become an instrument almost in disuse, substituted for the modern firearms. But this wartime instrument nevertheless was studied for a long time by the artist and scientist in its mechanical elements (toothed wheel, springs, levers, cranks, arches), so much that he reserved them numerous pages of investigation in the Codex Atlanticus. The drawings enclosed in these two sheets enjoy great clarity and definition in the same technical complexity, even if Leonardo seems to be more involved in admiring the different use of springs, let alone the elasticity of the wood arms in strong tension, till folding on themselves in the sling catapults or with a more rigid position in those endowed with spoon, to estimate then their different propulsive thrust and the various potentialities in the throw of a body. In grace of the produced energy, the loaded projectile could be hurled at a great distance also for arsoning purposes.

MACHINE-GUN

c. 1482. Codex Atlanticus, f. 56 v [157 r]. Milan, Biblioteca Ambrosiana

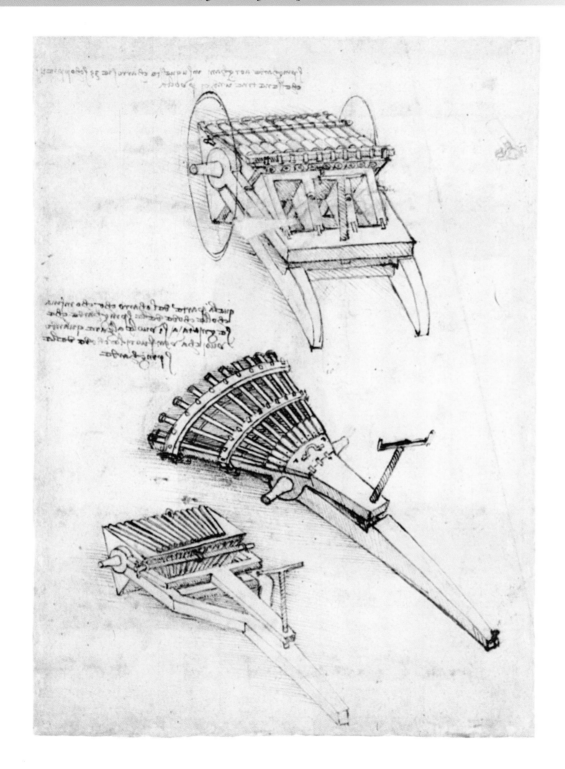

THE ELEGANT drawings of this sheet show some remarkable models of a machine-gun, suitable for demonstrating the innovation of the arms that Leonardo invented, that undoubtedly were placed in the vanguard of the military field and for such reason were destined to stimulate the interest of potential clients. The artist and scientist meant to submit his projects to some illustrious and powerful gentleman who might appreciate at last his manifold and exceptional abilities, as well as his technical knowledge, in the art of war. The two circles traced around the machine and hardly perceivable, suggesting their dimension and the possibility of a movement of the firearm in the battlefield, allowed to observe the loading system. These examples of light artillery were supplied of machine-guns with barrels disposed like in a fan, as the "springald with organs", that, though complicated in the loading of the projectiles, with three revolving racks, on which there were mounted "33 fusils", could guarantee, simultaneously or singularly, uninterrupted fire. The shooting sight was regulated from a worm screw, which made the machine take different inclinations for the angle of throw.

COVERED CART
FOR ATTACKING WALLS

c. 1480. Codex Atlanticus, f. 391 v-a [1084 r]. Milan, Biblioteca Ambrosiana

ALWAYS CONNECTED with the image of the military creativity of Leonardo as an engineer it is his juvenile conceiving of this war machine. Resumed from ancient times, it is equipped with wheels and is moved by means of animal force, in order to favour the approach of the soldiers to the walls and their making an assault on a castle. The large siege machine, in virtue of its mobility, leans against the enemy walls a long horizontal armoured bridge with a triangular cover, thus allowing the armed men to exceed the impediment of a defensive ditch and to reach unharmed the enemy positions.

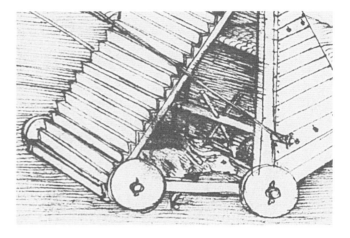

NAVAL CANNON

c. 1483-85. Windsor, RL 12652

AT THE END of the fifteenth century, the interest for the firearms and their improvement began to be more and more insistent, as they had become the fundamental instruments of the military art and the decisive elements for the destiny of battles. Leonardo had written to the Moor that he knew how to construct a variety of machines of great effectiveness, suitable to offence and defence also in any possible war at sea: "And when it should happen to be at sea, I have many instruments the most appropriate to offend and to defend, and ships that will make resistance to the shooting of all with a most large bombard and powder and smoke". This assertion is developed by the artist in the representation of the naval cannon, constituted from a single mortar mounted on the revolving platform of a boat and manoeuvred from a single sailor-artilleryman, that, using a mixture of powder and resin, following the Byzantine use, causes great amounts of smoke and pours an infinity of projectiles towards the enemy ships.

OGIVAL
PROJECTILES

c. 1508. Codex Arundel, f. 54 r. London, British Library

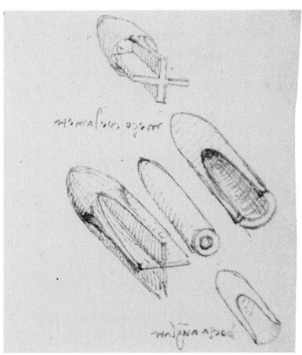

AROUND 1500, comes back to Leonardo the old passion of the military engineer and his interests are focused on new ideas for a fortified architecture (star-shaped plan of a city with angled bastions) as well as studies on ballistics, revealing the evolution of his researches on war instruments and on everything that was related to the art of war, as the optimal shape to confer to projectiles, the incidence of projectiles on masonries, the possible cover of the shooting field (Codex L, ff. 43 *v*; 45 *v*). Studies of ballistics which are farther on increased when, in 1502, received the assignment of "architect and general engineer" of the Duke Valentino, he is in

the retinue of the army of Cesare Borgia through Tuscany, Marches and Romagna (1502). Leonardo, having understood the correlation existing between water and air and having examined the movement of a body in a fluid, senses that the balls hurled from the cannons are influenced in their trajectory by the presence of air. Therefore, in the attempt to improve the precision of shooting of his firearms, he discovers that the pointed shape of the front part of a projectile would have favoured the aerodynamic penetration of the device, stabilizing its trajectory. Therefore, just in this sheet of the Arundel (f. 54 *r*), he draws and plans ogival projectiles, that turn out to be of incredible modernity both for their aerodynamic shape and for the equipment of the directional fins.

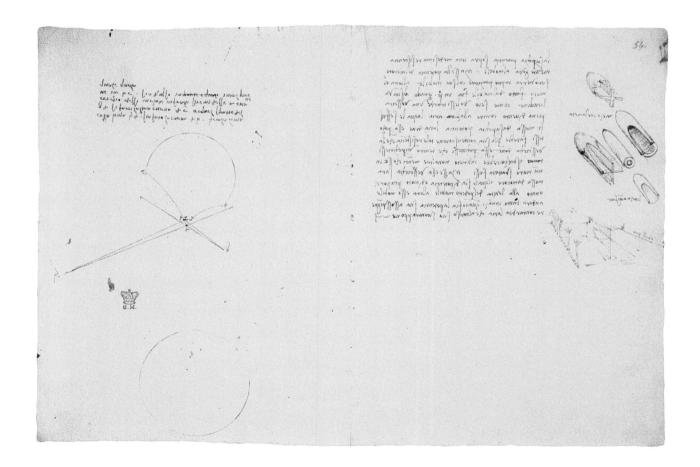

STEAM CANNON

c. 1482. Codex B, f. 33 r. Paris, Institut de France

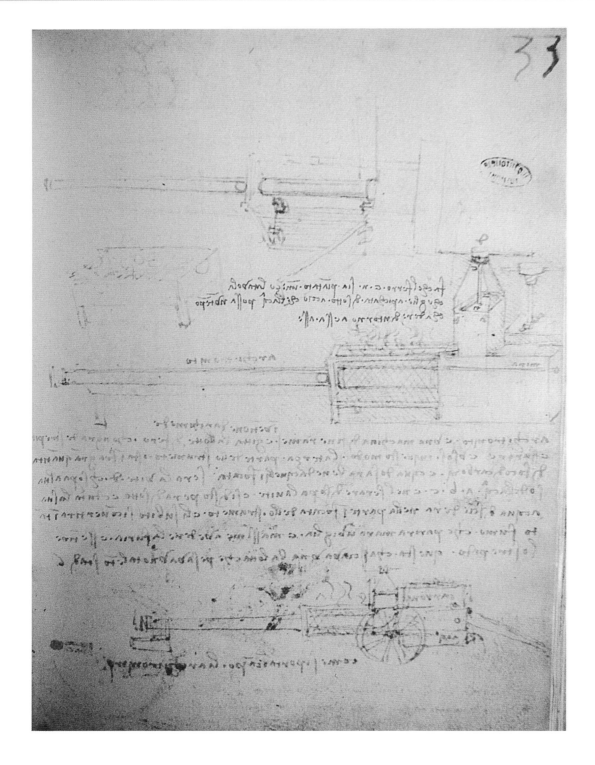

IN MODERN wars, infantry in the end supplanted cavalry, the use of swords and spears was replaced by light firearms like the harquebuses and by the cannons, of which were studied the systems of sight and of throw in order to inflict greater losses to the enemy on the field or to rip open the walls of their towns. Leonardo devised daring solutions also for the cannon, making no more use of gunpowder, but using steam. An invention that Leonardo said he had borrowed from the study of the great Syracusan scientist Archimedes, maybe through the Petrarch or perhaps through a source not confirmed, as it could be the humanist Guglielmo di Pastrengo. For such a reason, in the attempt to cause amazement for the sensational effects produced on the visual and auditory ground ("to see and to hear"), considered the smoke and the roar, and the forecast of unimaginable devastations, called this new arm of his "architronitus": a cannon equipped with wheels, to favour its positioning, and with an haulage bar, so that it could be moved along the plans, sometimes steep and impassable, of a battlefield. On the breech of this cannon, heated by a burning brazier, and made red-hot for the high temperature, was poured abundant water. The unexpected pressure of steam thus created would have made the projectile leave, hurling it to a great distance: "Immediately it will convert into so much smoke that it will appear to be a wonder; and moreover seeing the fury and hearing the roar". The steam cannon (Winans) would have been constructed and used in the second half of the nineteenth century, during the American civil war.

TECHNIQUES
OF ASSAULT

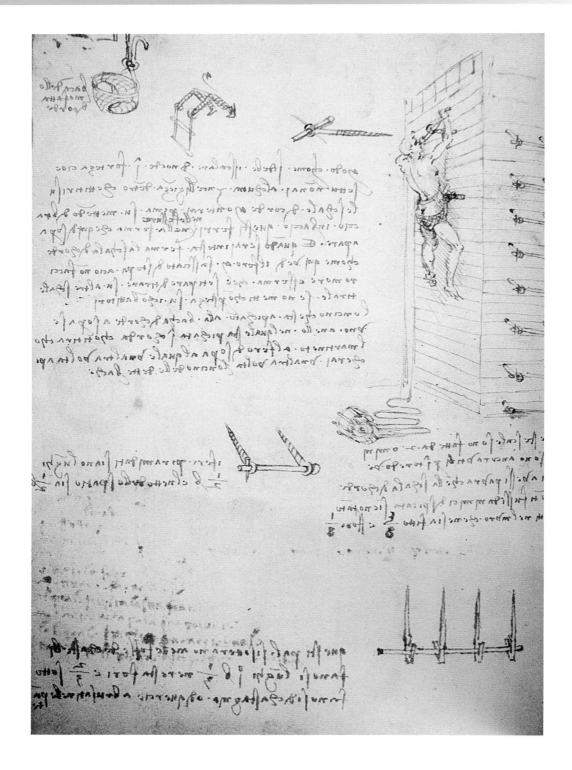

AFTER HAVING designed numerous instruments and a multiple variety of rope and wood ladders (mobile ladders [Forster Codex I, f. 46 *v*] and ladders for onslaught [CA, f. 868 *v*]), which to make use of to conquer in a direct way the walls of a fortress, Leonardo lingers to describe other systems and techniques of onslaught, drawing an athletic human figure, that, with coordinated movements, carries on a vertical scaling of the wall curtain of a building, with a simplified formal structure, making use of his own muscular force and of harpoons he has to implant steadly in the spaces among the bricks, in order then to favour the fast rise of other fellow soldiers.

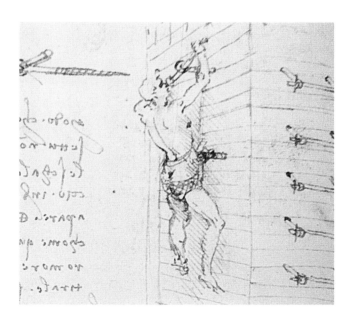

BOAT
WITH SCYTHE

c. 1484-86. Ashburnham Codex 2037, f. 8 r. Paris, Bibliothèque Nationale

THINKING OF war at sea, even before having recourse to fortified boats equipped with easy to use firearms, Leonardo resumed from roman naval engineering the idea to construct particular boats equipped with gigantic scythes with devastating effects and aimed at cutting trees and sails of the enemy ships, in order then to cause their sinking.

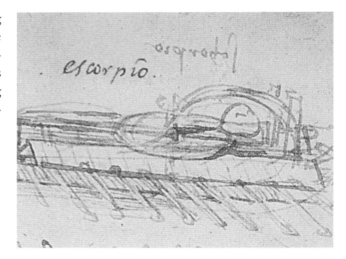

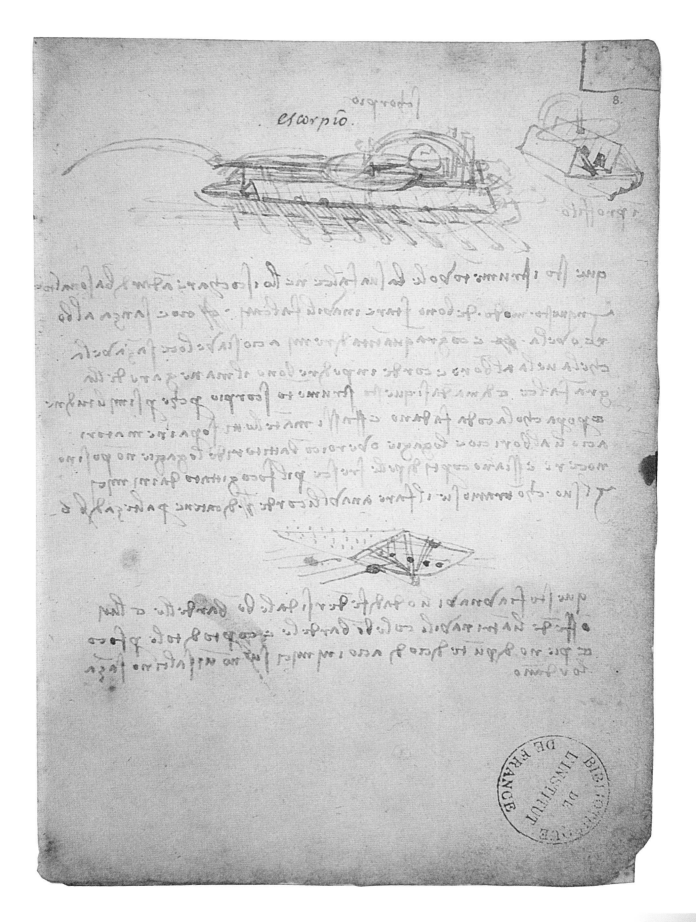

TANK

c. 1483-85. Inv. n. 1860-6-16-99. London, British Museum

IN THE FAMOUS letter sent to Ludovico the Moor (ab. 1482-83) and included in a sheet of the Codex Atlanticus (f. 391 *r-a*), Leonardo exalts his extraordinary ability as military engineer, able to devise and to construct also terrible war machines. Enumerating these competences, in the seventh sentence, he declares he knows how to realize "covered wagons, safe and invulnerable, which entering through the enemies with its artilleries, there is not any (large) great multitude of armed people that we could not break off, and behind these there will be able to follow many infantries, unharmed and without any obstacle". The artist-scientist meant to construct a covered heavy wagon, whose external struc-

ture was shaped like the armoured shell of a turtle, provided with a sighting turret. In this way, acting the dorsal part as a protection shield, this had to be covered for greater sturdiness with metallic plates, while in the part below the entire perimeter of the armour had to be mounted and to be dislocated a series of guns, capable of shooting in every direction and to carry out a fire of cover or a fire to dismantle the enemy lines ("This is good to break off their formations but it needs continuation"). The movement of the machine, represented turned upside down in the figure on the left in order to reveal its inner structure, was entrusted to a complex system of gears, connecting between themselves the drive

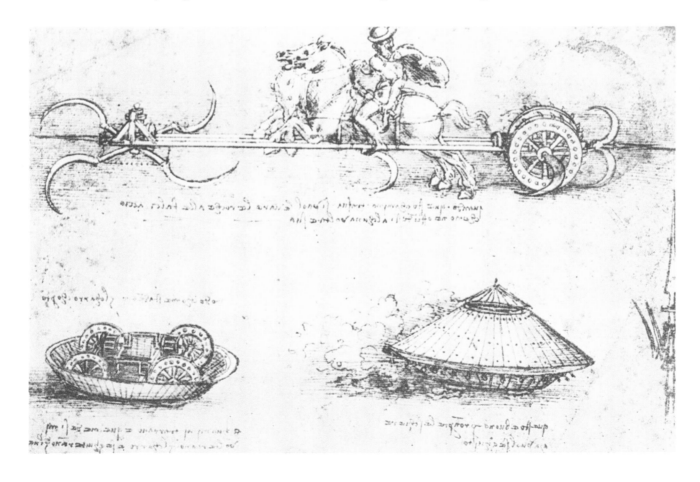

wheels, while it is believed that "8 men" would have made it work, setting in action some cranks. The interest borrowed to the study of the mechanics and the motor system, in any case connected to a theoretical and practical knowledge, had led Leonardo to exceed on the creative ground the traditional position of the medieval and contemporary artist-engineers, which had assumed for their war machines a motion by sail or the use of oxen or of horses. On the other hand, the use of horses, lodged inside the tank, for the transport of the machine in a battlefield, it had seemed to him to be at all inopportune and not trustworthy, because the explosions and the roar of the projectiles of the cannons would have made them become restive, until making them unmanageable and disobedient to whichever planned strategy.

CART WITH SCYTHES
TO MOW DOWN

c. 1485. Inv. n. 15583. Turin, Biblioteca Reale

THE CART with scythes to mow down, as a terrifying and deadly war machine, did not constitute in the fifteenth century any particular innovation in the field of military engineering, as it already existed in the classical ages since the time of the Romans. It is Leonardo in person who emphasizes its remote invention: "these carts were of various ways and often they made more damage to friends than to enemies [...] against these carts must be used archers, catapultists and launchers and throwers in every which way of darts, spears, stones, fires, beating of drums, shouting [...] and all of this will give scare to the horses which unbridled will turn themselves much to the irritation of their governors". A description of the cart with scythes to mow down had been carried out by Vitruvius (*De Architectura*), one of the so much admired *auctores* of the first Renaissance, but perhaps Leonardo had examined it in the *De Re Militari* by Roberto Valturio (Madrid Code II, ff. 2 *v*-3 *r*), in the popularized translation made by Paolo Ramusio published in Verona, in 1483, from where he would have also derived the present military vocabulary in the Codex B of the Institut de France (1485-90) as well as in the Codex Trivulzianus (c. 1490). The related drawings of Leonardo about the cart with scythes to mow down, preceded by the sketches made in the Codex B

(f. 10 *r*), illustrate with the effectiveness of an extraordinary visual language the devastating and "spectacular" effects caused by the rotating and well sharpened scythes, that mutilate the bodies of the enemies as a tender harvest. The scene is of intense dramatic effect and seems to anticipate, participating of a single mental speech ("describe" and "represent") and of the interactive function of his observations of mechanics, anatomy and physiognomics, the denunciation he made of war as "the most beastly madness", that will animate, in his bringing man near to beast, those junctions of bodies and limbs of the *Battle of Anghiari* (1503-04). In the two drawings of Turin, even the horses and the men participate of the same furious sudden impetus, nearly forgetting or at least taking into the background every interest for the technological aspects of the carts. However, Leonardo examined them, to demonstrate his preparation and his effective interest for the instruments and the war machines already matured in his practice of "workshop" in the years spent in Florence. A cart, with toothed wheels and pegs, was led by a pair of galloping horses, which concurred to transmit the rotating motion to the gear of the main cage, on which two rotating blades were mounted, with a deterrent function for the approach of the enemies also from the back, while through a long driving shaft a rotating motion was impressed also to the front system, that therefore would have set in action other four deadly rotating scythes. The operation of these machines, as of many others, it is however defective; and Leonardo was well aware of it, since he meant to preserve in this way the secret of his inventions, in the event his papers had reached other people's hands.

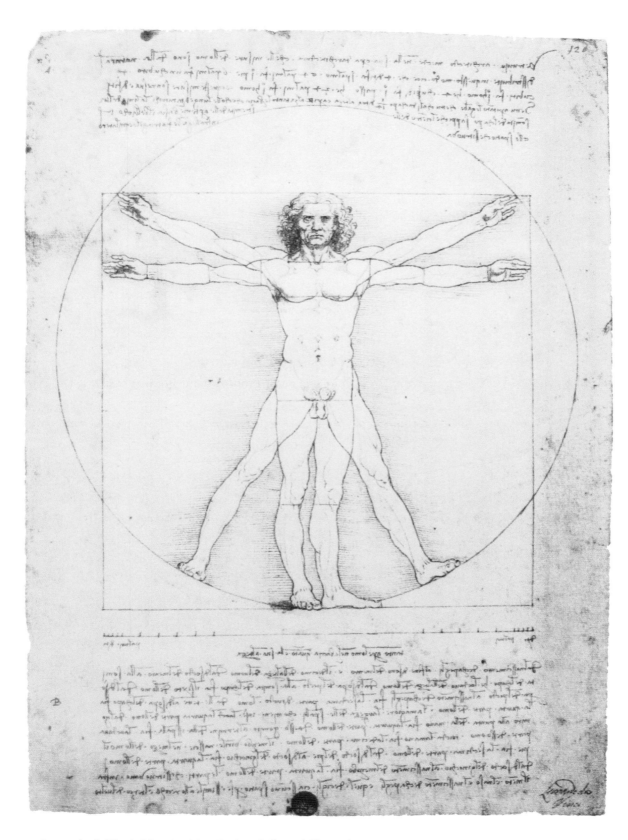

Leonardo da Vinci, *Vitruvian Man*. Venice, Gallerie dell'Accademia, n. 228

BIBLIOGRAPHY

ALBERTI DE MAZZERI S., *Leonardo. L'uomo e il suo tempo*, Milano, Rusconi, 1983.

AMORETTI C., *Memorie storiche su la vita, gli studj e le opere di Lionardo da Vinci*, in *Trattato della Pittura*, Milano, Editori de' Classici italiani, 1804.

ANGIOLILLO M. L., *Leonardo. Feste e teatri*, presentazione di C. Pedretti, Napoli, Società Editrice Napoletana, 1979.

ARASSE D., *Léonard de Vinci. Le rythme du monde*, Paris, Hazan, 1997.

BABINGER F., *Eine Brücke von Galata nach Stambul: wollte Leonardo in die Dienste des Sultans treten?*, «Die neue Zeitung», 87-88 (1952).

BARATTA M., *Leonardo da Vinci negli studi per la navigazione dell'Arno*, «Bollettino della Società Geografica Italiana», VI, 10-11 (1905).

BECK T., *Beiträge zur geschichte des Machinenbaues*, Berlin, Springer, 1900.

BELTRAMI L., *L'aeroplano di Leonardo*, in *Leonardo da Vinci. Conferenze fiorentine*, Milano, Treves 1910.

BELTRAMI L., *Leonardo da Vinci e l'aviazione*, Milano, Allegretti, 1912.

CALVI G., *Vita di Leonardo*, Brescia, Morcelliana, 1936.

CALVI I., *L'ingegneria militare di Leonardo*, Mostra della Scienza e della Tecnica di Leonardo presso il Museo Nazionale della Scienza e della Tecnica, Milano, 1952.

CAMPIONI R., *Leonardo artista delle macchine e cartografo* (a cura di), presentazione di C. Pedretti, Firenze, Giunti, 1994.

CANESTRINI G., *Leonardo costruttore di Macchine e di veicoli*, Milano-Roma, Tumminelli, 1939.

CARPICECI M., *I meccanismi musicali di Leonardo*, «Raccolta Vinciana», XXII (1987).

CHASTEL A., GALLUZZI P., PEDRETTI C., *Leonardo*, «Art Dossier», 12, Firenze, Giunti, 1987.

CIANCHI M., *Le macchine di Leonardo*, introduzione di C. Pedretti, Firenze, Becocci, 1982.

CLAYTON M., *Leonardo da Vinci. One hundred Drawings from the collection of Her Majesty the Queen*, London, Merrell Holberton, 1997.

COOPER M., *The Inventions of Leonardo da Vinci*, New York, The MacMillan Co., 1965.

CREMANTE S., *Leonardo da Vinci, genio delle macchine* (a cura di). Introduzione di M. Lombardi e Presentazione di C. Pedretti, Firenze, Cartei & Becagli, 2005.

DE TONI N., *Frammenti Vinciani XXVI: Contributo alla conoscenza dei Manoscritti 8936 ed 8937 della Biblioteca Nazionale di Madrid*, «Commentari dell'Ateneo di Brescia per il 1966» (ristampato in «Physis», 1, IX, 1967).

ESCOBAR S., *Il tecnico idraulico tra sapere e saper fare*, in *Leonardo e le vie dell'acqua*, Firenze, Giunti Barbèra, 1983.

FAVARO A., *Archimede e Leonardo da Vinci*, «Atti del Regio Istituto Veneto di Scienze, Lettere ed Arti», LXXVII (1917).

FIRPO L., *Leonardo architetto e urbanista*, Torino, UTET, 1971.

FIRPO L., *Leonardo architetto militare e civile*, «Lettura Vinciana», XVI, Firenze, Giunti Barbèra, 1976.

GALDI G. P., *Leonardo's Helicopter and Archimedes' Screw: the Principle of Action and Reaction*, «Achademia Leonardi Vinci. Journal of Leonardo Studies and Bibliography of Vinciana», IV, Firenze, Giunti, 1991

GALLUZZI P., *La carrière d'un technologue*, in *Léonard de Vinci ingénieur et architecte*, introduction de C. Pedretti, catalogo della mostra, Montréal, Musée des Beaux-Arts, 1987.

GALLUZZI P., *Prima di Leonardo. Cultura delle macchine a Siena nel Rinascimento*, Milano, Electa, 1991.

GALLUZZI P., *Gli ingegneri del Rinascimento, da Brunelleschi a Leonardo da Vinci*, Firenze, Giunti, 1996.

GIACOMELLI R., *Leonardo da Vinci e il volo meccanico*, «L'Aerotecnica», VI, 1927.

GIACOMELLI R., *Gli scritti di Leonardo da Vinci sul volo*, Roma, Bardi, 1936.

GIACOMELLI R., *Leonardo da Vinci aerodinamico, aerologo, aerotecnico ed osservatore del volo degli uccelli*, «Atti del Convegno di Studi Vinciani», Firenze, Olschki, 1953.

GIBBS-SMITH C. H., *Leonardo da Vinci's Aeronautics*, London, H.M.S.O., 1967.

GIBBS-SMITH C. H., *Le invenzioni di Leonardo*, Milano, Mazzotta, 1979.

GIBBS-SMITH C. H., *Aviation. An Historical Survey from its Origins to the End of World War*, II, London, HMSO, 1985.

GILLE B., *Leonardo e gli ingegneri del Rinascimento*, Milano, Feltrinelli, 1972.

HART I. B., *Leonardo da Vinci as a Pioneer of Aviation*, «The Journal of the Royal Aeronautical Society», XXVII (1923).

HERZFELD M., *La rappresentazione della 'Danae' organizzata da Leonardo*, «Raccolta Vinciana», XI (1920-22).

HEYDENREICH L. H., *L'architetto militare*, in *Leonardo inventore*, Firenze, Giunti Barbèra, 1981.

KEMP M., *Leonardo da Vinci. Le mirabili operazioni della natura e dell'uomo*, Milano, Mondadori, 1982.

KEMP M., *Leonardo's Fossils*, «Natural History», CV, 11 (1996).

LAURENZA D., *Gli studi leonardiani sul volo. Spunti per una riconsiderazione*, in *Tutte le opere non son per stancarmi. Raccolta di scritti per i settant'anni di Carlo Pedretti*, a cura di F. Frosini, Roma, Edizioni Associate, 1998.

LAURENZA D., *Leonardo. Il volo*, Firenze, Giunti, 2004.

LAURENZA D., *Le Macchine di Leonardo. Segreti e invenzioni nei Codici da Vinci*, a cura di M. Taddei e E. Zanon, Firenze, Giunti, 2005.

LIGABUE G., *Leonardo da Vinci e i fossili*, Vicenza, Neri Pozza, 1977.

MARANI P. C., *L'architettura fortificata negli studi di Leonardo da Vinci*, Firenze, Olschki, 1984.

MARANI P. C., *'Circulo dentato ortogonialmente' (Ms. Madrid 8937, f. 117r). Leonardo, gli ingegneri e alcune macchine lombarde*, «Lettura Vinciana», XXV, Firenze, Giunti Barbèra, 1985.

MARCOLONGO R., *Le invenzioni di Leonardo da Vinci.*

Parte prima, Opere idrauliche, aviazione, «Scientia», 41, 180 (1927).

MARCOLONGO R., *Leonardo da Vinci artista-scienziato*, Milano, Hoepli, 1943.

MARINONI A., *Codice Atlantico*, trascrizione diplomatica e critica 12 voll. (a cura di), Firenze, Giunti, 1975-80.

MARINONI A., *Gli scritti di Leonardo*, in *Leonardo scienziato*, Firenze, Giunti Barbèra, 1980.

MAZENTA G. A., *Le memorie su Leonardo da Vinci di Don Ambrogio Mazenta ripubblicate ed illustrate da D. Luigi Gramatica*, Milano, Alfieri & Lacroix, 1919.

MAZZOCCHI DOGLIO M., *Leonardo 'apparatore' di spettacoli a Milano*, in *Leonardo e gli spettacoli del suo tempo*, catalogo della mostra, Milano, Electa, 1983.

MCMAHON A. PH., *Leonardo da Vinci: Treatise on Painting*, introduction by L. H. Heydenreich, Princeton University Press, 1956.

MIGLIORE S., *Tra Hermes e Prometeo. Il mito di Leonardo nel Decadentismo europeo*, Firenze, Olschki, 1994.

PEDRETTI C., *Macchine volanti inedite di Leonardo*, «Ali», 3 (1953).

PEDRETTI C., *Spigolature aeronautiche vinciane*, «Raccolta Vinciana», XVII (1954).

PEDRETTI C., *La macchina idraulica costruita da Leonardo per conto di Bernardo Rucellai e i primi contatori d'acqua*, «Raccolta Vinciana», XVII (1954).

PEDRETTI C., *L'elicottero*, in *Studi Vinciani*, Genève, Droz, 1957.

PEDRETTI C., *Leonardo at Lyon*, «Raccolta Vinciana», XIX (1962).

PEDRETTI C., *Dessins d'une scène, exécutés par Léonard de Vinci pour Charles d'Amboise (1506-1507)*, in *Le lieu théâtral à la Renaissance*, Royaumont 22-27 marzo, Paris, CNRS, 1964.

PEDRETTI C., *Commentary to J. P. Richter's of the Literary Works*, Oxford, Phaidon, 1977.

PEDRETTI C., *Leonardo architetto*, Milano, Electa, 1978.

PEDRETTI C., *The Codex Atlanticus of Leonardo da Vinci. A Catalogue of its Newly Restored Sheets*, 2 vols, New York, Johnson Reprint Corporation, Harcourt Brace Jovanovich, 1978.

PEDRETTI C., *Leonardo: Il Codice Hammer e la mappa di*

Imola. Arte e scienza a Bologna, in Emilia e Romagna nel primo Cinquecento (a cura di), Firenze, Giunti Barbèra, 1985.

PEDRETTI C., *The Gaddi 'puella'*, «Achademia Leonardi Vinci. Journal of Leonardo Studies and Bibliography of Vinciana», IV, Firenze, Giunti, 1991.

PEDRETTI C., *Leonardo's Robot*, «Achademia Leonardi Vinci. Journal of Leonardo Studies and Bibliography of Vinciana», X, Firenze, Giunti, 1997.

PEDRETTI C., *Il teatrino di Leonardo*, «Il Sole-24 Ore. Domenica», 27 giugno 1999.

PEDRETTI C., *Leonardo. Le macchine*, Firenze, Giunti, 1999.

PEDRETTI C., *Leonardo da Vinci. La Battaglia di Anghiari e le armi sofisticate*, Firenze, Grantour, 2000.

PEDRETTI C., *Presentazione*, in *Leonardo da Vinci. Il codice Atlantico della Biblioteca Ambrosiana di Milano nella trascrizione critica di Augusto Marinoni*, Firenze, Giunti, 2000.

PEDRETTI C., CIANCHI M., *Leonardo. I codici*, «Art Dossier», 100, Firenze, Giunti, 1995.

PEDRETTI C., VECCE C., *Libro di Pittura. Codice Urbinate lat. 1270 nella Biblioteca Apostolica Vaticana*, Firenze, Giunti, 1995.

PEDRETTI C., VECCE C., *Leonardo da Vinci. Il Codice Arundel 263 nella British Library. Edizione in fac-simile nel riordinamento cronologico dei suoi fascicoli*, Firenze, Giunti, 1998.

PIDCOCK M., *The Hang Glider*, «Achademia Leonardi Vinci. Journal of Leonardo Studies and Bibliography of Vinciana», VI, Firenze, Giunti, 1993.

PIUMATI G., *Il codice Atlantico di Leonardo da Vinci nella Biblioteca Ambrosiana di Milano, riprodotto e pubblicato dalla Regia Accademia dei Lincei. Trascrizione diplomatica e critica di G. Piumati*, prefazione di F. Briosi, Milano, Hoepli, 1894-1903.

PIUMATI G., SABACHNIKOFF T., *Codice sul volo degli uccelli e varie altre materie* (a cura di), trad. di Ch. Ravaisson-Mollien, Paris, Rouveyre, 1893.

POPHAM A. E., *The Drawings of Leonardo da Vinci*, London, Cape, 1946.

POPHAM A. E., *Leonardo's Drawings at Windsor*, «Atti del Convegno di Studi Vinciani», Firenze, Olschki, 1953.

PRAZ M., *Leonardo in Inghilterra*, «Ulisse», V, 17 (1952-53).

RAVAISSON MOLLIEN CH., *Les manuscrits de Léonard de Vinci*, Paris, Quantin, 1881-1891.

REGTEREN ALTENA VAN J., *Rubens as a Draughtsman, I, Relations with Italian Art*, «Burlington Magazine», LXXVI (1940).

RETI L., *Helicopters and Whirligigs*, «Raccolta Vinciana», XX (1964).

RETI L., *The Two Unpublished Manuscripts of Leonardo da Vinci in the Biblioteca Nacional of Madrid*, «Burlington Magazine», CX (1964).

RETI L., *Tracce di progetti perduti di Filippo Brunelleschi nel Codice Atlantico di Leonardo da Vinci*, «Lettura Vinciana», IV, Firenze, Giunti Barbèra, 1965.

RETI L., *The Leonardo da Vinci Codices in the Biblioteca Nacional of Madrid*, «Technology and Culture», VIII (1967).

RICHTER J. P., *The Literary Works of Leonardo da Vinci Compiled and Edited from the Original Manuscripts* (edited by), 2 vols, London, Low-Marston-Searle and Rivington, 1883, *Commentary* by C. PEDRETTI, Oxford, Phaidon, 1977.

ROBERTS J., *Il Codice Hammer di Leonardo da Vinci* (a cura di), presentazione di C. Pedretti, Firenze, Giunti Barbèra, 1982.

ROBERTS J., *Master Drawings in the Royal Collection: from Leonardo da Vinci to the present day*, London, Collins Harvill in association with The Queen's Gallery, 1986.

ROSHEIM M. E., *L'automa programmabile di Leonardo*, «Lettura Vinciana», XL, Firenze, Giunti, 2001.

SCAGLIA G., *Alle origini degli studi tecnologici di Leonardo: la sega idraulica e le macchine per la palla e croce*, «Lettura Vinciana», XX, Firenze, Giunti Barbèra, 1981.

SEMENZA G., *L'automobile di Leonardo*, «Archeion», IX, 1 (1928).

STARNAZZI C., *Leonardo. Acque e terre*, presentazione di C. Pedretti, libro-catalogo e mostra a Cesenatico a cura di C. Starnazzi, 6 luglio-8 settembre, Firenze, Grantour, 2002.

STARNAZZI C., *Studio per l'Orfeo del Poliziano. Una questione di meccanica applicata*, in *Leonardo da Vinci. Il Foglio del teatro*, catalogo e mostra a cura di C. Starnazzi, Arezzo, 1 giugno-30 settembre, Arezzo, Badiali, 2002.

STARNAZZI C., *Scenografie per Charles d'Amboise, gover-*

natore di Milano, in *Leonardo da Vinci. Il Foglio del teatro*, catalogo e mostra a cura di C. Starnazzi, Arezzo, 1 giugno-30 settembre, Arezzo, Badiali, 2002.

STARNAZZI C., *Leonardo cartografo*, Firenze, I. G. M., 2003.

STEINITZ K. T., *Le dessin de Léonard de Vinci pour la représentation de la Danae de Baldassarre Taccone*, in *Le lieu théâtral à la Renaissance*, Royaumont 22-27 mars, Paris, CNRS, 1964.

STEINITZ K. T., *Leonardo architetto teatrale e organizzatore di feste*, «Lettura Vinciana», IX, Firenze, Giunti Barbèra, 1969.

SUTERA S., *Leonardo. Le fantastiche macchine di Leonardo da Vinci al Museo Nazionale della Scienza e della Tecnologia di Milano. Disegni e modelli*, Milano, 2001.

TISSONI BENVENUTI A., *Il teatro volgare della Milano sforzesca*, in *Milano nell'età di Ludovico il Moro*. «Atti del Convegno Internazionale», 28 febbraio-4 marzo 1983, Milano, Il Comune: Archivio storico civico e Biblioteca Trivulziana, 1983.

TURSINI L., *Le armi di Leonardo da Vinci*, Milano, Mostra della Scienza e della Tecnica di Leonardo presso il Museo Nazionale della Scienza e della Tecnica di Milano, 1952.

UCCELLI A., *Leonardo e l'automobile*, «Raccolta Vinciana», XV-XVI (1935-1939).

UCCELLI A., *Leonardo da Vinci. I libri di meccanica, nella rivoluzione ordinata di A. Uccelli*, Milano, Hoepli, 1940.

UCCELLI A., ZAMMATTIO C., *I libri del volo di Leonardo da Vinci*, Milano, Hoepli, 1952.

VECCE C., *Leonardo*, Roma, Salerno, 1998.

VERGA E., *Bibliografia vinciana, 1493-1930*, 2 voll., Bologna, Zanichelli, 1931.

VEZZOSI A., *Leonardo da Vinci. Arte e scienza dell' universo*, Milano-Parigi, Electa/Gallimard, 1996.

WINTERNITZ E., *Leonardo da Vinci as a Musician*, New Haven, Yale University Press, 1982.

ZAMMATTIO C., *Gli studi di Leonardo da Vinci sul volo*, «Pirelli», IV, 1951.

ZAMMATTIO C., *Acque e Pietre: loro meccanica*, in *Leonardo scienziato*, Firenze, Giunti Barbèra, 1981.

ZÖLLNER F., *Rubens Rework Leonardo: "The Fight for the Standard"*, «Achademia Leonardi Vinci. Journal of Leonardo Studies and Bibliography of Vinciana», IV, Firenze, Giunti, 1991.

ZUFFI S., *Leonardo da Vinci. Della natura, peso e moto delle acque. Il Codice Leicester* (a cura di), presentazione di F. Zeri, Milano, Electa, 1995.

Lombard Anonymous of the Fifteenth Century,
Emblem of the Leonardo Academy, *c.* 1495.
Milan, Biblioteca Ambrosiana, n. 9596e.

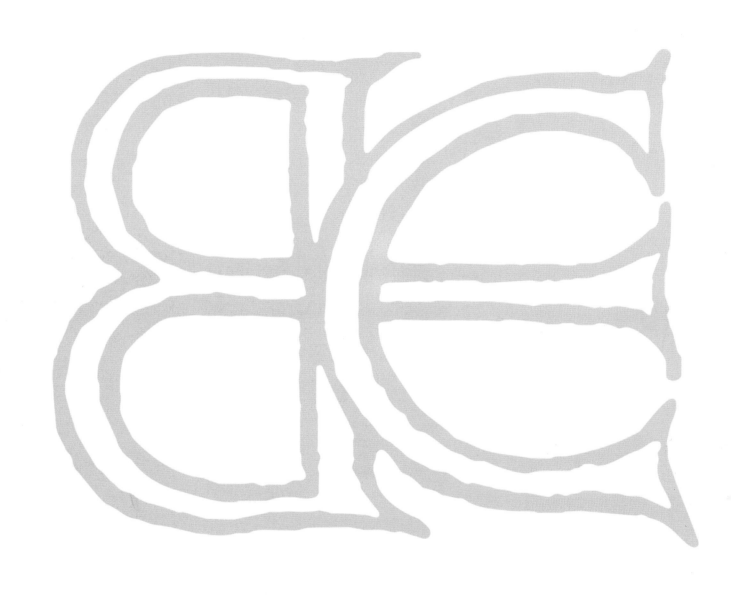

Printed in the month of October 2006
at New Color of Florence
for Cartei & Bianchi Editors